UNCOMMON SENSE

The Roadmap
to a Great
Business Board

MICHAEL GIVONI

Copyright © Michael Givoni 2022
Contact: www.boardapproach.com.au
Melbourne, Australia
Title: *Uncommon Sense – The Roadmap to a Great Business Board*
Author: Michael Givoni
ISBN: 9780645455700
Business | Management | Strategy
Book Production: www.bevryanpublish.com

A catalogue record for this
book is available from the
National Library of Australia

NATIONAL
LIBRARY
OF AUSTRALIA

Dedication

This book is dedicated to my father,
Don Givoni, who is 96 years young this year.

Born into a Warsaw domiciled Polish family, and emigrating
to Melbourne in the 1930s, Dad built a prominent textile
manufacturing business under the Givoni brand.

Empathy and loyalty, such as that shown by
Dad towards his staff, is and always will be the
cornerstone of great family businesses.

Contents

Introduction

Uncommon Sense is a book about boards, but not as you know them. It has not been written from the point of view of formal governance, or through a legal lens, or from a fiduciary duty, compliance or risk-mitigation perspective. These elements are important, but there are many other books and articles that deal with them in fine detail.

Rather, the book provides a practical perspective to maximising the effectiveness of the boards of privately owned, small- to mid-size enterprises (SME) in Australia. It will also resonate with owners of small cap-listed companies. The book shows the pivotal role that boards play in steering shareholders towards achieving their objectives—once those objectives are understood. In almost every situation, a board's primary role is to increase the value of the business for its owners.

Uncommon Sense will also help explain that making money is certainly not an evil objective. In fact, the world of contemporary governance, and social and environmental expectations, can exist comfortably within a board's primary-shareholder, value-creating objectives.

We have a special affinity with the founding or entrepreneurial phase of the business cycle, where a 'family table' format may need to transition to a fully functioning board. The founders may have started their business in the garage or post-grad classroom, or a few like-minded members of a family or friendship group may have built their business based on a fabulous idea.

Fast forward a few years to where the business has grown significantly, however, and there may be a sense of unease, a sense of loss of capacity to keep control of the beast. There may be advisers and peers endlessly counselling the founders on managing further growth in a controlled manner, and on the need for structure, and a leadership framework for effective decision-making may even be urgent. At this point it's time to consider a governance function for the corporation, i.e. a board.

There are a few excellent books on the topic of boards, but the vast majority of them (and especially the well-written ones) lean heavily on examples drawn from the world of Australian Securities Exchange (ASX) top-200 companies. There is much insight to be gleaned from these case studies and books; however, most of the advice is tailored to those who want to play an important role on existing boards for large and predominantly listed companies. This book will sit comfortably on the shelf next to these other publications, but its focus and intended audience are very different.

Most of the advice in this book is for business founders and owners who want to either establish a high-functioning board or turn an underperforming board into an excellent one. If you are founding a board or improving an existing one, this book will help you do that. It will also support aspiring, new and existing directors in improving their leadership skills and their approach to handling matters of the board.

Uncommon Sense is the product of the author's almost forty years of experience. Most of the business owners that have been helped by the approach outlined in these pages run businesses that generate $20–100 million in turnover and $3–15 million in profit, i.e. mid-market, and private family businesses.

The size of your company may present certain limitations that make other books on this subject less helpful than this one. For instance, you might not have access to a pool of former CEOs and board members who have occupied corner offices at global brands like GM, GE, and IBM. Your company might be too small to attract the notice of the biggest of the big hitters, so advice drawn from that world won't apply to your situation. While it's possible to learn from those companies' successes and mistakes, their experiences and the contexts in which they operate may not be aligned with your own circumstances.

Hopefully, many of the practical steps in this book will seem like common sense to founders and private-company owners. In a world of political correctness, common sense is fast becoming less common. The knowledge in this book should demystify the role of a board, and inspire you, the reader, to establish a highly effective board, leading to even greater commercial outcomes.

Chapter 1
THE TIPPING POINT

At some stage in a private company's journey there will be a tipping point where a high-performing board can play a pivotal role in navigating the next phase of growth. This is the point in the journey where founders must consider letting go and recognising that sustainability for the business could be beyond their omnipresent fingerprints.

Many business owners whose boards have benefitted from the approach contained in this book made their first appearance in a boardroom on the day they established a board for their own business. Some owners may have reported to boards when they were younger corporate citizens, but their entrepreneurial spirit has since led them out of the corporate world and into the sphere of business ownership. The central part of this book's thesis is that the founder's/owner's objectives are pivotal to strategy. Owners who have built successful enterprises, often from the ground up, will eventually ask themselves: *What should I do with the business? What is the end game?*

Establishing a board will help refine, and strategically bring to fruition, ultimate objectives. There are typically five options a board can use to help owners make a decision about where to take their business:

1. Hold on to the company, remaining as CEO/chair at the head of the organisation well into retirement.
2. Transfer control of the company to the next generation, keeping control of the company in the family.
3. Facilitate the entry of younger members of the executive team so they can buy in and gradually assume control of the company.
4. Sell the company, usually to either a private equity (PE) firm or a competitor.
5. Take the company public.

A high-functioning board should play a key role in a company, from its inception to driving towards one of these five chosen end-game objectives (examples of which are included throughout the book). The owners are the board's servants, after all. A fundamental fact (almost always forgotten) is that the primary role of a board and its chair is to help the owners steer their business towards their desired end-game objective within an agreed timeframe. However, the primary issue of growth and exit rarely appear on the typical board's agenda.

The shape and composition of the board will also depend on which of the five above options is chosen. In the unique thesis presented in this book, a highly effective board should openly explore each option at the very outset of the board's formation, or when a new, independent chair is in situ. This allows the board to explore the timing and price expectation on exit; that is, the chair needs to gain a sense of the business's current valuation, thereafter providing a high-level road map to exit, including identifying any obvious gaps.

If you're holding on to the company, the right board will help your business reach that mature corporate stage, with a disciplined governance structure and a clear vision for the future. If you're transferring the company as a legacy to the next generation, you'll be handing off something both valuable and lasting. Mentoring the next generation becomes a priority task. If you're selling the business to PE, or taking the company public, a vastly different approach is required. Long-term strategic options need to be developed, with a fresh, energised executive team (outside of the founder group) that is ready, willing and able to execute. It's about leaving plenty of firepower and growth momentum for the next round of owners.

So the task of establishing the best board for the business must be approached methodologically, seriously and energetically, with the same kind of entrepreneurial spirit that drove the founders to establish and grow the business in the first place. That's what is meant by the phrase 'working *on* it' rather than 'working *in* it'.

A culturally aligned board, with objectives that are tangible, can reenergise a business, injecting into the mix new and diverse thinking, insights and experiences. It will serve as a powerful bridge connecting ownership to management. If driven by a skilled, independent chair—resisted by many founders who want to keep control of the organisation—it will bring with it clear optionality.

Trust is central, the glue that binds the board together. Psychological safety is a crucial element of trust; that is, the comfort derived from the ability to be wrong, or to make mistakes in front of one's team. Research shows that teams (including boards) see 'higher levels of engagement, increased motivation to tackle difficult problems, more learning and development opportunities, and better performance' when members trust each other and feel psychologically safe.[1] This comes down to the 'essentials of human relationships relating to the three core drivers of trust: authenticity, logic, and empathy. People tend to trust you when they think they are interacting with the real you (authenticity), when they have faith in your judgement and competence (logic), and when they believe that you care about them (empathy)'.[2]

BRINGING IN THE RIGHT PEOPLE

Choosing the right independent chair is an important first step. Developing a deep relationship of trust and respect between chair and founders/owners, and thereafter chair and management, is a sacrosanct part of our thesis in this book. Once that contract of trust exists between the board chair and the key stakeholders, the other pieces of the board puzzle can be put into place. Analogous to a music band, the members in the board 'band' all have an important role to play in the ensemble, and must be playing the same tune, with the chair as lead conductor.

Trust, psychological safety and mutual respect are all vital for a smoothly functioning board. It takes time to build the rhythm, and we provide some simple tools to support that process. Board-performance evaluation is also essential, and the tools included in the book will help keep the focus on the overarching strategic objectives.

Increasingly important are also the non-financial and sometimes non-tangible considerations, which are vital enablers. These include leadership and culture, the social context, diversity, equity, and inclusion. In the book we consider some of the policies required to support the board and the business to be responsible corporate citizens in the increasing acknowledgement that business can be utilised as a tool for social good, and for solving some of the world's seemingly inextricable and complex challenges.

None of this will happen overnight. It requires clarity regarding objectives, and a deliberate, disciplined approach over a number of years to take the business to where the owner wants it to be, with the financial and social impact that the owner wants to see. It requires trust, a long-term strategic plan, and clearly identified successorship in senior-management ranks so a prospective buyer will have reason to invest, support and enhance the pre-existing process for the next stage of the business's evolution.

The book will help business owners learn to let go; help define the distinction between owners, boards and management; and help chairs find and keep their good directors through this evolutionary but potentially disruptive period.

My interest in board effectiveness, and its role in extending the entrepreneurial spirit well beyond the founders' phase, began with the fifteen years I spent as an executive at Spotless Group, an iconic Melbourne-headquartered ASX-listed company. The founder, Ian McMullin, founded a drycleaning retail chain, and the next group of leaders, Ron Evans and Brian Blythe, extended the business into contract catering and facility management. The entrepreneurial leadership and energy, lasting some fifty years, was based on family values and was operated by a loyal executive team with skin in the game. In recent years the business was acquired by engineering group, Downer, and its halcyon days are arguably behind it. Yet it's a wonderful case study of how a well-led board can continue to extend the founders' vision.

THE BENEFITS OF A MID-MARKET PRIVATE BOARD

In a large, top-100 ASX company the CEO wields significant power and influence. The CEO retains consultants to design the strategy, the big four for audit and tax, and international law firms for legal issues, all at a huge cost. The CEO brings strategy to the board for ratification. However, all these advisors have loyalty to the CEO, who in turn is accountable to the board's chair, which means the ASX top-100 non-executive directors have far less influence on future prospects of the business than outsiders might presume.

In mid-sized private or family businesses, the chair and board must do far more of the heavy lifting themselves because more often than not the business cannot afford to outsource these critical tasks to skilled external consultants. The board must shape strategy, address gaps in capability, ensure transparency in data, build successorship, mitigate risk, and drive growth initiatives. These are the key enablers to deliver the desired exit strategy.

The board works to make the company more valuable for the owners/shareholders. Our approach in this book is to focus on the exit strategy, and not simply compliance for compliance's sake. Compliance (and the board-approved governance policies that follow) is an important by-product of the legislative settings of the day. It's about being a responsible corporate citizen in a particular legal, social, financial, risk, and reporting context. Failure to have regard for these contemporary issues can and will destroy reputations, which in turn can erode the very shareholder value the board has been driving to build. A high-functioning board must have due regard for these compliance issues, plus sound risk frameworks.

High-functioning boards are the exception, not the rule. A board's purpose is to drive the creation of shareholder value, and some boards do this poorly or not at all. Rather than shaping the company's vision for the future, the board may be taking precise measurements of the ground beneath its feet. Rather than addressing issues once and for all, they may be simply rubberstamping them. These boards are simply tidying around the fringes and going through the motions. They may be compliant, and they may be fulfilling their mandate, but they're not doing what boards can and should do, mostly because the owners are not entirely aware of how to properly establish, manage and utilise their board or its governance function.

A great board doesn't happen by accident. It's the product of careful planning and equally careful execution. Corporate governance is rarely thought of as an electrifying subject, but some of the most engaging conversations on this subject have centred on the potential for boards to be powerful leadership vehicles.

KEY TAKEAWAYS

✓ Culturally aligned boards with objectives that are tangible and measurable can reenergise a business, injecting new, diverse thinking and experience into the mix.

✓ Boards serve as powerful bridges connecting ownership to management, and driven by a skilled independent chair will bring clear optionality.

✓ Trust is central, the glue that binds the board together.

✓ Boards help refine and bring to fruition the owners' ultimate objectives, which are typically limited to five options:

1. Hold on to the company well into retirement.
2. Transfer to a next-generation successor.
3. Facilitate management buy-in.
4. Sell the company, either to a private equity firm, family office or competitor.
5. Take the company public.

Chapter 2
WHY DO BOARDS EXIST?

Ask even an experienced director why there are boards, and they'll probably share their thoughts on what boards are good for, which wouldn't really answer the question. They might talk about compliance or management oversight, but that would only explain what a board does and not why it does it. The concept of a board is a late-nineteenth-century innovation. The word 'board' is often used interchangeably with the terms 'corporate oversight' or 'corporate governance'. The concept of corporate governance is fraught with inconsistencies about what that actually encapsulates. Are boards about compliance and accountability, or growth and risk? Are they about good corporate citizenship, or shared purpose; or all of the above?

MANY HEADS ARE BETTER THAN ONE

It can be helpful to look at examples of early boards of governors. During the Middle Ages, communities of tradespeople banded together and appointed groups of men, who met semi-regularly, to make important decisions on their communities' behalf. Using a broad definition, these could be seen as the earliest examples of corporate boards, although realistically the concerns of modern corporations and those of mediaeval guilds and feudal city states don't share much in common.

Those concerns started to converge in the sixteenth century, when English merchants, given royal licence to operate in the Orient, or the New World, started expanding in size and power. In 1554, Queen Mary of England and her husband, Philip of Spain, signed a charter with an English trading enterprise, the Muscovy Company, granting the company a monopoly on trade between England and Russia. This was the first documented example of a 'joint stock company'; previously, rough collections of merchants had sailed under the same banner, each with their own stock. The members of the Muscovy Company subscribed to a fund that financed the purchase of goods. Those who contributed to this fund were—although they weren't yet called so—stockholders.

The Muscovy charter named Sebastian Cabot as governor for life, but it did more than this. It also appointed four 'sad, discreet, and honest' consuls and twenty-four assistants to these men. It's not the company itself that is interesting, but the appointment of the four sad, discreet, and honest men to oversee it, implying as it does that the men had to be of a certain character and disposition; not only honest but also serious and able to keep a confidence.

These same three descriptors appeared in corporate documents for centuries after the Muscovy charter. We see the same calls for a disciplined governing body in seventeenth-century charters outlining the demands of shareholders who had invested in the young colony that would one day become the United States. We see them again in the earliest bank charters in England and the United States, and we see them in the founding documents of some of the world's first truly corporate enterprises: The Levant Company (1592), the Hudson's Bay Company (1670), and the South Sea Company (1711). The last of these became the first example of a board of governors shirking responsibility when reckless speculation led to the spectacular collapse of the company, wiping out almost overnight the equivalent of trillions of dollars in today's money.[3]

The early history of corporate governance overflows with examples of poor and unethical oversight. Still, a guiding principle shines through in the documentation: boards were thought of as a way to ensure that the worst impulses of unscrupulous men of business would be checked. At least in the abstract, the evidence shows that when groups of people with vested economic interests pool resources (as shareholders still do), having a group of sober and judicious governors is more comforting than having only one single decision-maker such as a CEO, no matter how trustworthy.

With industrialisation, and the advent of modern companies that are a little more familiar, the regulatory environment necessitated the development of more disciplined governance structures. Following the management revolution of the 1930s, technocrats took the place of oligarchs and, for the first time, according to Charam, Carey, and Useem, 'expertise trumped pedigree'. Boards were at least starting to become what they could be.[4]

With increasing calls for accountability from the public, and pressure from major investors, this movement towards more responsible and leadership-oriented boards has accelerated in the twenty-first century. We are finally starting to be able to answer the question 'Why do we have boards?' without blushing. We have boards because we believe that oversight is necessary on behalf of ownership groups (shareholders/founders), and because we believe that a group of 'sad, discreet, and honest' professionals can make better decisions together than they can apart.

WORK *ON* THE BUSINESS, *NOT* IN IT

There is a second answer that can be given in response to the question of why we have boards. Boards exist so founders/owners can stop working *in* their business and start working *on* it. As we know, founders/owners can too easily be dragged into the busyness of business and away from the broader, vision-based decision-making aspect, and the challenges relating to changing trends in the market.

A high-functioning board allows founders/owners to truly work *on* the business. It provides a mechanism by which they can view their business in three dimensions: the day-to-day routine (tasks), the long-term business goals (strategy), and the even longer-term end goal (the business as a transferable asset). Most business owners only have time and space to think about the first two dimensions (tasks and strategy), and the investment decisions that go with each of those. A board, and particularly a carefully built board, is the means by which that three-dimensional picture starts to come into focus.

Working in the business is absolutely essential, but once the business has reached a sustainable scale, the founders/owners should be thinking about the future of the asset they have built and their roles within it. If, for example, an owner plans to sell the company before retiring, a relatively small investment in the board can make a significant, positive impact. A high-functioning board can often mean the difference between a tidy retirement nest egg and multi-generational wealth.

I am often asked what the threshold sustainable scale is, i.e. the best time for founders to start thinking about stepping back and using the vehicle of a high-functioning board to chart the next stage of growth for their business. It's usually when earnings are in the $3–5-million-per-annum bracket, and often coincides with other critical decisions facing owners. Appoint an outsider as CEO, and/or expand geographically into a new state or country? Grow organically, or contemplate an acquisition to fast track consolidation in the sector? These critical decisions signal that a business is readying to exit the founder phase and enter its next stage of entrepreneurial growth.

One of my most admired founders is Adelaide businessman Andrew Downs of Sage Automation. An electrical contractor by trade, Andrew built the business, yet made critical decisions that involved him letting go of absolute control. He set up an independent board, introduced a high-calibre CEO and CFO, and allowed key executive and board members to buy shares, thereby ensuring their alignment and long-term commitment, if not loyalty. Andrew still leads by example with ideas, sound counsel, and critical introductions. His business has gone from strength to strength, in no small part due to the courage he showed in letting go of control and empowering others to share in the journey.

WHEN A BOARD ISN'T A BOARD

There is a fair amount of confusion about the term 'board of directors'—what it actually means, and the kind of entities it applies to. A board is a collection of duly appointed directors that are formally appointed pursuant to the company constitution, with the associated paperwork lodged with the Australian Securities and Investments Commission.

It's worth noting that in closely held family companies, rather than muddying the lines between management, ownership and the board, the owners can make use of an advisory board. Advisory boards lack the formal authority and mandate to lead, but they can serve as sounding boards for the owners. There was a time when advisory boards were a way to insulate board members from serious consequences or even scrutiny: however, that time is behind us. If an advisory board starts to behave like a formal board, stakeholders and regulators will likely hold it accountable. If an advisory board's advice is at the centre of a catastrophe, it will be every bit as exposed as a formal board, which is why advisory-board members should ensure they are covered by directors' and officers' insurance policies, despite not being formally appointed as directors.

Boards can also have subcommittees that perform specialised functions once the size of the organisation justifies these deeper-dive interventions. These subcommittees often include audit-and-risk committees and remuneration committees, and usually comprise a mix of board members, but they also allow non-board members and experts in their fields to be included. Each subcommittee will have its own terms of reference and make recommendations to the full board to consider and ultimately endorse.

The word 'committee' is often used interchangeably with the word 'board'. The two are not the same and the distinction should be noted. Committees are usually the remit of charitable, sporting, or school-governing bodies. The function of a committee can be similar to that of a board, but committees are often less formal and comprise talented individuals who volunteer their time and expertise.

KEY TAKEAWAYS

✓ A board is a collection of duly appointed directors, formally appointed pursuant to the company's constitution.

✓ Boards exist so founders and owners can stop working *in* their business and start working *on* it.

✓ A board's primary role is to deliver on the owners' objectives in creating shareholder value.

✓ Boards provide a mechanism to view the business in three dimensions: day-to-day routine (tasks), long-term business goals (strategy), and even longer-term end goals (the business as a transferable asset).

✓ Owners sometimes make use of advisory boards, which, although lacking formal authority, can serve an important role for the owners.

Chapter 3
WHAT GREAT LOOKS LIKE: B.O.A.R.D.S.

If establishing a board that runs smoothly and achieves its objectives were easy, every company would have a high-functioning board with shareholders who are as pleased as punch. But that isn't the case. Boards present unique challenges to those who attempt to establish and chair them, and for those who sit on them. When these challenges are undertaken poorly (or not at all), the result is a broken board.

Many different criteria are recommended for the establishment of a successful board. Charan, Carey and Useem[5] summarise them well by suggesting that a well-led board should have the following attributes:

- Compelling central idea
- Board leader who organises and directs the board

- Board nomination and remuneration committee (this group sets the board and executive remuneration, and evaluates leadership performance, individually and collectively, across the organisation)
- Working partnership with top management
- Set of active directors with leadership experience
- Absence of dysfunctional directors
- Regular evaluation of directors and the board
- Set of protocols for making or delegating decisions
- Commitment to lead and not just monitor the company

There are specific governance recommendations and requirements for ASX companies (ASX Corporate Governance Council, ASX Corporate Governance Principles and Recommendations),[6] but these are guides for private and family businesses only, which are generally under less scrutiny.

At the mid-market private-business level, board members are custodians of the organisation's culture and values, and they should adhere to the behaviours inherent in the acronym B.O.A.R.D.S., which stands for: beyond reproach, objective, agile, risk-weighted, decision-makers, and stakeholders. We'll now take a closer look at each of these values.

BEYOND REPROACH

When thinking of acting beyond reproach, one naturally thinks of the legal duties of directors, and ongoing compliance with those obligations pertaining to directors enshrined in the *Corporations Act*. However, 'beyond reproach' is what the board, the chair and the whole organisation stand for. This raises the question of what the role of business is in society. Standing for something must be in line with societal contexts: environmental, social and governance, diversity and inclusion, shared value, integrated thinking, business for good, ethical supply chains, and wellbeing.

The business-judgement rule, which states that where care and rational judgement are applied to a circumstance that produces adverse results for a company, directors are to be protected from legal consequences, negligence in particular; however, there are other consequences to consider. Even if the board manages to wriggle its way out of a tight legal spot, the reputational consequences might be enough to tank the brand, and the organisation with it.

The solution to this is quite simple. Every decision the board makes has to be able to pass the public or 'glass box' test. It's not just about whether the board as a whole, and the individual directors, are comfortable with a decision; it's about how comfortable members of the board would be if the public could see into the boardroom and scrutinise its decisions. Board meetings may take place behind closed doors, but it can be instructive to think of the boardroom as a glass box. Crowded around the box, their noses pressed to the glass, are the employees and customers, and the broader public.

I think about every decision I make as a chair or a director like this: If this decision were splashed across the front page of tomorrow's paper, how would it look? How would somebody who has never heard of this company and the work it does see our actions today if they were told about them (either with or without context)? It's not only out-and-out villainy that needs to be rooted out; perceptions are crucial, and even if you can explain away the perception, the damage may have been done long before the company proffers its official excuses. How things look is important; bad optics means bad business.

If, as a director, you've looked the other way when the head of marketing set up a casting couch in his office, or if you've signed off on bribes in developing markets, would these actions pass the glass-box test? Of course not. No amount of explaining could make those stains come out in the wash. If you get caught utilising sweatshop labour, clearcutting the rainforest, or pouring pollutants into rivers, the tar will never come off—ever.

In 2021, CEO Christine Holgate provided a classic test case for a board where politics, ethics and claims of misogyny all converged in one episode. Her decision to hand out Cartier watches to management was a matter to be signed off by the board (explicitly or implicitly); the glass-box or public test may not have been proactively used by the directors at that time.

Closer to daily decision-making, conflict of interest and nepotism can be challenging for private companies and family businesses.

In closely held companies, conflicts of interest and nepotism are almost taken for granted. The owner's son-in-law works for a local law firm, so of course it's that law firm that represents the company. Despite joining the company only six months previously, the owner's younger brother is approved by the board for a senior-management role, overlooking more worthy employees. Neither of these scenarios would fly in companies with broadly spread ownership, but can be treated as normal in organisations where those who own and control the companies share a last name.

Even the glass-box test comes down to the owners' objectives. If the owners' overriding objective is to create long-term shareholder value, there is no room for nepotism. This is not to say that family interests and business interests can't be aligned; boards can often be a mechanism for owners to nurture the next generation. When there is merit at the core of each promotion—or a lack of it at the core of each termination—family and business interests can absolutely be one and the same.

Unwritten rules, especially in the murky waters of ethics, are essentially *optional* rules. Even if the members of the board are upstanding corporate citizens, even if they are family or long-time friends, it's imperative to put things in writing in a board charter. This is a sign of corporate maturity, and anything less than a documented code of conduct for the board will make experienced prospective board members think twice, and the same can be said for potential investors. This expands into the realm of the broader social purpose, which should be aligned with strategy. Code of conduct relates to behaviours, and board charter relates to objectives. They can be combined in one document, but we recommend they stay separate.

Far too few boards have a clear central idea that guides their deliberations. They might make an effort to adhere to the company's mission statement, but these statements are often too vague to be practical in the boardroom. High-functioning boards should always have clear guiding principles they can refer to whenever a decision has to be made about the company's long-term direction.

Dino Strano declared his vision in crystal-clear terms at our very first meeting. My role as chair was to navigate sustainable growth to accommodate the intergenerational objectives of the three children assuming key leadership roles over the next decade. Brandon Chizik at RSEA had equally clear objectives: put in place a board, and a management and funding structure, which would support a high-growth entrepreneurial business over the next decade. Graham Thomas, in his advancing years at Dutt Transport, had the stated objective of using an energised board to set up the business for trade sale or management buy-out. Three outstanding founders, but with differing objectives, and as a consequence the board is constituted with a charter that reaffirms the key objectives.

With a clear brief in hand from the owners, the chair should document a board charter: a concise summary of the overarching shareholder objectives, incorporating the leadership and behavioural traits to be adopted by the board in achieving those objectives. Frame the board charter and display it prominently as a useful reminder of the board's true purpose, and to serve as a reminder at board meetings of why the directors are there.

OBJECTIVE

Few things can reveal at a glance whether a board is set up for success or failure more than clarity on whether the board is seated at a table with four stable legs, as an independent, objective decision-making body:

- Leg one: The board is accountable to the owners/ founders for creating shareholder value and delivering on owner objectives.
- Leg two: The board is a decision-making body that delivers on owner objectives by providing management with oversight counsel and direction.
- Leg three: The CEO and management are responsible for the day-to-day operation of the business, using the parameters of delegation of authority issued by the board.
- Leg four: The board is led by an empathetic, capable, and independently-minded chairman.

When there are clear dividing lines between all four legs, and when the responsibilities of each are clearly defined, each leg can keep its focus on its priorities. For management, this means operational control; for ownership, it means sharpening the big picture, and providing clear and achievable long-term objectives; for the board, it means management oversight and transforming the goals of ownership into tangible strategies.

Early on in my career, I was a non-equity partner in an 18-partner law firm called Wisewoulds. It occurred to me then, and it still does today, what a challenge it is to run a business when the owners and major fee earners are one and the same. Great lawyers do not necessarily make the best CEOs or line managers. Professional-services professionals such as lawyers, accountants and architects often struggle with the dilemma of separation between owner and manager. Consequently the four legs of these board tables are not always stable.

The more the lines separating one from the other are blurred, the more difficult it will be for the board to act as the objective, independent, data-centric, deliberative, decision-making body it can and should be.

In order to grow the value for shareholders, one of the board's most important tasks is to sever the cord that connects management and ownership. A board acts as an independent intermediary, the conduit between the owners/founders and management. In closely held businesses, with ownership vested in the hands of a single individual or a small handful of people, this often means a dramatic change in the established order.

High-functioning chairs and boards should be independent of both management and ownership. When there is no separation (when, for instance, the owner is also the CEO, or chair, or even both), the business's fortunes are tethered to the owner. Client or vendor relationships are the owner's networks, and the company's fortunes rise or fall with the quality of those connections. As the owner ages, so too do those relationships.

My own family-business story is a case in point. My father was a visionary business leader and much loved by his staff. He built a five-factory network across Victoria, headquartered in Bay Road, Sandringham. Givoni Mills, at its essence, was a vertically integrated sleepwear manufacturer. At its height in the 1970s, Dad employed four hundred staff and had sophisticated plants that could knit, sow, quilt, dye, cut, and pack fabric into dressing gowns, robes, nightgowns and pyjamas. It was ahead of its time for design, and an early adopter in licensing international brands such as Playboy and Christian Dior.

The organisational design centred on the founder, my father. Four of my brothers worked in the business right through until the early 2000s. As my father aged, so too did his loyal customers, who frequented department stores such as Grace Brothers, Myer and David Jones.

The external threat was a global push towards free trade and lowered trade barriers, which meant that Australian manufacturing could not compete with low-wage countries such as

China and Bangladesh. Despite my father vigorously lobbying Canberra on behalf of the clothing and textile industry, it was a losing battle. A slow but inevitable wipeout of Victoria's textile manufacturing sector followed.

Could there have been a way for my father to pivot? He didn't really want to sell the business, and my brothers were entrenched in key roles. Knowing what I know now, I can see that a high-functioning board would and should have provided the sound counsel needed to leverage the excellent reputation of the business into new growth channels.

It would have needed a strong, talented and trusted independent chair to convince my father to invest in these new areas, such as online sales and his own chain of retail stores. After all, the business's DNA was as a contract manufacturer, yet it needed to become a house of brands, with sales and marketing (online/retail direct) as its core competency, which would have meant a huge cultural mindset shift. No doubt my father would have made this shift had he been the beneficiary of the trusted and talented resources around him at board level.

The window to transform the business model did pass, which was no tragedy, by the way, as the baton of the business was transferred to two of my brothers when my father retired. His legacy was profound.

What can be learned from my own family's experience and many other similar stories of that era? Strong, patriarchal-style founders who build and closely control their operations can sometimes be unaware of outside threats, or worse, underestimate their impact. Also, a strong founding figurehead can often struggle to find executives willing and able to challenge and robustly debate issues, much to the detriment of long-term planning and a clear exit path.

The board's position as a bridge between ownership and management can only be effective if the board chair is truly independent and objective.

In my first board meeting with Graham Thomas, the owner of Dutt Logistics, he asked me to set up his business for exit one day, either by trade sale, private equity (PE), or management buy-out. Graham was in his late seventies, unwell and no longer active in the business. He was astute, and a keen student of economics, especially the disciplines of EVA (economic value add, using weighted average cost of capital as key indices to evaluate performance).

Twenty years earlier, Graham had put his faith in Peter Davies as CEO, a shrewd move. The two characters were oil and water, but Peter had done a stunning job of building the business to be a highly respected and profitable logistics organisation. It's now a major supplier to Coles and Cotton On, among others.

Early board meetings are my way of assessing how realistic owners' objectives are, and identifying the gaps to execute. To my mind, key early questions are: Is the management team that's in place doing the best job they can with what they've been given to work with? Do they have the right tools and the right training to address the problems they're facing?

In this case, the foundations were very sound. Customer retention was high, safety standards were embedded, and the plant (fleet of trucks and warehouse facilities) was well maintained. Yet a few pieces of the puzzle were missing. There needed to be better reporting and transparency on key data at board level, and also evidence of a growth strategy, supported by a sales-and-marketing capability.

There were three people on the board, so as a circuit breaker I added a fourth member, someone who was a new CFO. CFO Ashley immediately improved the board deck, and papers came to the board monthly. This freed up CEO Peter from being grilled on numbers, and he could focus on what he enjoyed and did superbly: manage customers and drive operations.

Once an independent chair has added value and proves that the board gets things right more often than not, the contract of trust can be built. A high-functioning and objective board is the very best management-consulting vehicle invented.

Within a board, there should be input from differing perspectives, offered without fear of reprisal, even when there is potential conflict with other perspectives at the table. There should be robust debate surrounding key issues, but this debate needs to be respectful and to lead somewhere. There should also be diversity of experience and opinion within the individuals, who can collaborate and reach consensus.

If some directors think a given course of action is absolutely the wrong move, an enlightened chair won't plough through on the strength of the numbers being on their side. They will discuss the evidence and dispel doubts with data-centric proof and without emotion. There should never be a member of the board who asks to have it recorded that they're abstaining or dissenting from the board's decision. Although this might indicate a red flag for the individual, more often it indicates a red flag for the decision that is about to be made, or for the evidence presented. Stated reservations are different, but they should be able to support the decision, even with those reservations.

A board stacked with people who have the same background means they share a common set of lenses through which they see the world. Having the same kind of people on a board just leads to the same results. If you're trying to look in new directions, diversity will help you see what you're missing. Merit should still be the first thing that's sought in a candidate, but after that, seek ways to grow your board by addition (not through multiplication). If a director adds the same value as the person seated to their left or right, they're not really adding anything.

All else being equal, who is the best fit for the role? Remember that sexism and racism is often subtle, lurking behind excuses like 'She would be a distraction' or 'He won't be taken seriously'. If you find yourself making excuses like this, ask yourself whether you're perpetuating the systems that have led to the boardroom being a white-male-dominated space.

The economic argument for diversity is loud and clear, with diverse voices at the table contributing to innovation, better risk management, and increased profit margins. However, the risk with diversity for the sake of diversity, across all the intersectionalities (gender, ethnicity, sexuality, age, race, disability) is that it is tokenistic. The best people should be retained based on merit, and that inclusion—where people feel free to voice their opinions and have agency in that process—does not develop solely as a result of the diversity of seats at the table.

AGILE

A strong bias to quick action is essential for a board to maximise opportunities, as they arise, to increase shareholder value. This is especially true in the mid-private-market board, where the role of chair is instrumental in extending the founder phase of a business life-cycle, and building on this entrepreneurial spirit while slowly assembling the framework for scalability, including better systems, people and governance.

Organisational agility breeds enthusiasm. When an opportunity presents itself, the board has a responsibility to quickly assess the risks and act at the most opportune time. Business is about *taking* risks, not *managing* them. Adaptive, agile resilience is key.

High-functioning boards see an opportunity, measure its distance and leap. They don't stand on the edge, look down at the water below, and wonder out loud whether what looks like logs are actually crocodiles. They have confidence in their judgement. They know whether they can take the landing or not. This is about holding on to get through challenging situations. Business is, by definition, unpredictable.

Taking on a role as chair does not just mean attending a monthly meeting, and hence a twelve-day-a-year engagement. It's not something to be slotted in around golf on Wednesday and long Collins St lunches on Friday. For me, it's a full-time career. It's my job. The businesses involved run 24/7 and so must the chair. I call it 'owners' mentality'. Think and act like an owner. That's how you run a board.

I may be at odds, being against this mantra of 'independent non-executive' chair that is considered best practice across Australia. I want agility and entrepreneurial behaviour on my boards, and so do the founders and shareholders I'm accountable to. Alignment of interest will always beat independence as a concept. That's why owners and investors such as PE firms encourage the chair, CEOs, and others in the leadership team to buy shares in their companies. It's not a gift, not a long-term incentive program—put your hand in your pocket and pay up.

There are situations where companies could facilitate the purchase of shares through shareholder loans, and could proactively assist those key leaders who do want to invest and make a long-term contribution. However, it's important for people to make a personal contribution to the investment. That's true alignment at every level, and that's what builds owners' mentality throughout the board and leadership, which can extend and sustain the founders' entrepreneurial spirit for the next phase of growth.

Chair and fellow board members, if totally aligned, will make themselves available whenever possible. When the

phone rings on a Saturday or Sunday, high-performing directors take the call, and they'll drop everything if the issue
demands an immediate response. When there's a problem,
they'll bring in the right people and handle the issue in a
way that leaves no doubt about their concern or resolve.
By setting the standard in this way, they foster an adaptive
and resilient culture. Nimble boards lead nimble companies.

High-functioning boards bring this curious, entrepreneurial
mindset to bear on critical questions around growing the
business and increasing value. This mindset includes people
who have real energy and a growth mindset. They are comfortable with taking risks, and have a bias towards positive decision-making and positive ideas. They are alert to external
trends in the marketplace, and want to make a difference to
the growth of the business. These are people who are forever
thinking, always wanting to grow and build things.

The following are typical discussions that should emerge around
the mid-market private-board table:

- Have fresh markets opened up interstate or overseas
  that call for an aggressive expansion into new territo-
  ries, and do we have the talent to enter these emerging
  markets?
- Has a new market entrant disrupted the way business
  is conducted, and if so, are we nimble enough to
  respond?

- Is our market share and new-product innovation likely to stagnate, and if so, will a change of management address this issue, or do we have a larger problem with our business model?

In an article by Gino Chirio,[7] he looks at how companies grow, and establishes that there are six broad ways:

1. New processes: Sell the same stuff at higher margins. Cut production and delivery costs, automate for efficiencies, cut fat in the supply chain or manufacturing, and utilise robots.
2. New experiences: Sell more of the same stuff to the same people. Increase retention and share by powerfully connecting with customers.
3. New features: Sell enhanced stuff to the same people. Add improvements that drive incremental purchases.
4. New customers: Sell more of the same stuff to new people. Introduce the product to new markets that have needs similar to your core, or to markets where it might address a different need.
5. New offerings: Make new stuff to sell. Develop a new product, not just enhancements. Find new needs to solve within existing markets, or invest in a new category.
6. New models: Sell stuff in a new way. Reimagine how to go to market by creating new revenue streams, channels, and ways of creating value.

Deciding which ways to grow needs to be intentional and strategic. Being agile is key. Stunting or stifling growth through creeping risk aversion around the board table is a founder's greatest fear.

RISK-WEIGHTED

A leadership team, which is what a board should function as, never has perfect information. After all, decision-making at board level means taking a series of calculated and measured risks. Risk-taking is the essence of business leadership. Embracing it, and developing expertise at pricing and assessing business risks, is an essential role of the board. Every decision, and every change, has an inherent risk. Investing time, money and resources on a business idea is the ultimate risk.

Risk cannot be eliminated in business, and taking measured calculated risk within a robust decision-making process that accounts for these is a vital function of a board. Often, this means decision-making with imperfect and incomplete information. Entrepreneurs are the ultimate intuitive risk-takers. Every risk has a price. Pharmaceutical companies take massive investment risks in a time-based race to patent new drugs. Mining companies spend zillions hoping the cost of extracting a given mineral, in a given country, allows a margin relative to the global commodity price at that time.

These all involve making courageous business decisions that lean on sophisticated data collection, modelling and forecasts.

Yet even with the most sophisticated financial models, and Harvard MBA executive horsepower, these key decisions are made by boards with imperfect information, and rely on a range of assumptions that may or may not prove to be factual. It is the work of the board to embrace risk-taking and become an effective decision-making body, even in the absence of complete and accurate data.

Risk is not a company's enemy, but its friend. Risk is certainly not hidden in some compliance register developed by the chief risk officer. Business growth is about pricing risks, not subcontracting out risks to some team or department on the side.

Risk is the essence of business. High-functioning boards are risk-takers, because that's the underlying imperative behind growing a profitable business in a competitive economy. Evaluate competing risks, weigh them and make a call. Transparency is key here. There is no right decision, just an optimal one with regard to the available information.

Boards evaluate and price risk. A high-performing board doesn't leap at every danger that presents itself as a possible opportunity, but it doesn't stick its tail between its legs either. It weighs risk carefully, examining the possible consequences and the likelihood that the gambit will pay out.

When establishing a board, directors should be people with a weighted risk-taking track record, and therefore a bias toward appointing commercial operators; they have run their own businesses, or a business division within a large corporation. If they can demonstrate that they can keep their cool and make the right choices when the stakes are at their highest, they probably have a knack for risk-pricing and risk-weighting. An entirely unblemished record is a sign that someone might price risk too highly. If fortune's wheel has always turned in their favour, chances are they will only give it a spin when the stakes are low.

Non-entrepreneurial risks are those without tangible financial rewards attached to them. They include safety risks, and risks to society and the planet that jeopardise the company's reputation. Consequences can be dire if these are avoided or ignored, or if the company simply gets by with the bare minimum, meeting the basic legal requirements.

The board should spend a considerable amount of time ensuring that there are policies in place to protect the company from all manner of threats, but the board's attention should be focused on the top-right quadrant, where consequences and probability are both high.

If, for instance, the company is a law firm, physical-safety risks will be extremely low, but risks surrounding mental health and sexual harassment will likely exist and must be handled delicately; whereas if the company is a mining group, physical safety and environmental risks will be paramount.

Risk weighting does not mean that only immediately relevant risks with severe consequences get the board's attention; it simply means that the board spends an appropriate amount of time analysing and bracing for risks of all kinds. If the potential rewards or the likelihood of risks are low, the time investment should be correspondingly less. We cannot and should not try to eliminate risk.

The board that doesn't assess risks in this way will have its back to the entrepreneurial winds. High-functioning boards turn their faces into these same winds, scenting opportunities that the risk-averse miss.

DECISION-MAKERS

Decision-making is about practice and boundaries. High-performing boards draw a clear line between decisions for management and decisions for the board. The board should apply its energies to the decisions for which they alone are responsible, delegating everything else to capable managers. Formally documented and published "delegations of authority" are critical to the playbook of the chair (on behalf of the board) and the CEO (on behalf of management) respectively.

The other repository of rules of engagement for the board is the shareholders' agreement. This is an agreement that sets out on behalf of shareholders what authority the board has, and which decisions they are happy for the board to make, and which decisions must come back to shareholders for approval at an extraordinary general meeting.

The chair has one clear focus of accountability, and that accountability is to the owners. The decisions the board can make from month to month reside in the shareholders' agreement, or, in the absence of an agreement, the company constitution. Armed with that knowledge, the chair creates a delegation-of-authority document for the CEO so they can run the business effectively, and only reverts to the board for major decisions, as prescribed in this delegations document.

Take a business with a turnover of around $30 million, with profits in the $3–5 million annualised range. Often the delegation line has a clear dollar figure attached to it. For example, any major expenditure under, say, $250,000, could be handled by the CEO and the executive team. Any investment decisions over this amount, including decisions regarding acquisitions or divestments, should be elevated to the board.

 The board should, however, always concern itself with approving annual budgets, determining the scope for external auditors, setting CEO and direct report remuneration, and signing the annual audited accounts.

Broader than decision-making, leadership is a force that can make or break the culture in any organisation. There is a plethora of material on leadership to help individuals determine the framework in which they lead. Adaptive, inclusive, servant, creative, ethical, and strategic leadership all have mountains of research dedicated to developing robust frameworks.

To be a director, or lead a board, a certain kind of business leadership is required, which includes an entrepreneurial spirit, a willingness to take risks, and a critical, analytical approach balanced with creativity. Underlying this is the business case for curiosity. Research suggests that cultivating curiosity helps 'leaders and their employees adapt to uncertain market conditions and external pressures: When our curiosity is triggered, we think more deeply and rationally about decisions and come up with more-creative solutions. In addition, curiosity allows leaders to gain more respect from their followers and inspires employees to develop more-trusting and more-collaborative relationships with colleagues'.[8]

Early on in my career, my mentors were partners in a law firm, namely Ben Frenkel and George Kefford. I saw them as wise, worldly men. They had lunch every day in a restaurant in Hardware Lane, sharing a permanent table with eminent Queen's Counsels and Supreme Court judges. Whilst I was clearly out of my league as a third- or fourth-year solicitor, I was never made to feel uncomfortable. I listened and learned how they saw and solved problems. I am grateful to Ben and George for including me. Watching and learning from outstanding problem-solvers cannot be taught in a classroom. Exercising sound judgement is also a skill that cannot be acquired working from a home office. These skills are acquired in a lifelong journey of interactions with more senior leaders who are willing to take an interest in your career development.

Keeping pace with changing societal expectations is now a critical focus for the chair and board. I was recently asked to provide counsel to a key member of an executive team accused of bullying. Bullying is a most serious matter and totally unacceptable. In this case, the individual concerned had issues outside the workplace that were impacting his performance in the office environment. No one incident was a sackable offence, but there was a chain of events that warranted intervention. We moved this high performer into a different role once he was prepared to own up to the stress he was under and acknowledge the impact he was having on others. On investigation, it was found that the situation could be dealt with proactively while preserving the dignity and reputations of both subjects and the accused. I was proud that the organisation I chaired was open and able to give someone a second chance.

STAKEHOLDERS

A contemporary and ever-increasing challenge for businesses is the plethora of social issues that now need to be taken into account, including the extent to which businesses must take a leadership role in social and environmental issues.

The influx of next-generation employees means this is an issue that mid-market private companies are increasingly facing. In my experience, this is very frustrating for many founders and private-company owners. The frustration does not come from a lack of care or interest in these issues; it's more to do with the additional investment in time and cost involved in addressing such issues, a burden that seems to have fallen at the feet of business owners and their representative boards.

Yet all the elements of successful boards are particularly important when looking beyond the financial outcomes of the business to the non-financial, sustainable value that a corporation can bring over the longer term, and how sustainability is embedded in every part of the business.

'It is ultimately the responsibility of the board to govern and strategically direct the organisation to perform in an accountable manner. While some governance failures come to light as realised financial risk events (such as capital and solvency issues), many more failures represent non-financial risk exposures, which may receive less attention in organisations. It is often not until conduct-related outcomes of poor governance come to light in a very public and reputationally damaging manner that the importance of strong corporate governance is realised'.[9]

Through this process we understand that it is a broader concept of stakeholders, including communities and the planet, as well as all the stakeholders in the supply chain, that the modern business boards are now being asked to give serious regard to.

Another theme that is emerging from the literature on boards and their value is the role of business for social good, and the responsibility that companies have to make a difference in areas of ethics, society and sustainability. From social corporate governance to shared value and everything in between, there is increasing pressure for companies of all sizes to be able to design, implement and measure their activities around impact. Business as an agent of social change—positive businesses, business for good being good for business—move to shared creation from doing no harm to playing an active role in solving environmental, social, and economic problems.[10]

In his paper 'The changing role of business in society', Michael Porter[11] summarises the evolution of responsibility:

- Shareholder primacy: The social responsibility of business is to increase its profits for shareholders.
- Corporate social responsibility: Compliance with ethical and community standards, good corporate citizenship, sustainability initiatives, mitigating risk and harm, improving trust and reputation.
- Corporate purpose: Addressing the question of why the company exists reflects the broader approach to making purpose powerful through addressing social issues. Purpose is reflected in culture and embedded operations.
- Stakeholder capitalism: Broader groups of stake-holders, including employees, customers, communities, suppliers and the environment, and not just shareholders.
- Creating shared value: Companies can meet societal needs with a profitable business model.
- Business and agents for positive social change.
- Positive business: The study of positive institutions based on the work of positive psychology, resilient institutions.

The evolving nature of business and its role in society means that boards need to have a broader understanding of the societal and environmental context in which they operate.

The Business Council of Australia champions the role that responsible businesses play in generating sustainable economic growth. 'We believe the role of business is to generate returns for shareholders over the medium to long term, and that doing this requires businesses to be good corporate citizens, and for big and small business to work together across our cities and regions … and balance the needs of all stakeholders and interests including employees, shareholders, customers, suppliers, the community and the environment'.[12]

There does need to be acknowledgement of the possible conflict between short-term financial gains and longer-term societal gains. Over the longer term, the companies that consider positive outcomes for all stakeholders are more likely to generate longer-term value in financial and societal-value creation. Boards are crucial in terms of guiding the material considerations that show contribution beyond financial value.

KEY TAKEAWAYS

The following characteristics are always part of great boards (B.O.A.R.D.S.):

✓ Beyond reproach: Boards must set the standards for the company in terms of values, ethics, culture and behaviour.

✓ Objective: Boards act as independent, data-centric, deliberate actors, creating a necessary bridge between ownership and management.

✓ Agile: A strong bias to action is essential for a board to optimise opportunities that come before it.

✓ Risk-weighted: All decision-making involves a series of calculated and measured risks; risk-taking is the essence of business leaderships.

✓ Decision-makers: High-performing boards draw a clear distinction between decisions for management and decisions for the board. The demarcation of responsibility is outlined in the delegations of authority (responsibilities of management delegated by board) and the shareholders' agreement (responsibilities of the board delegated by the owner).

✓ Stakeholders: Successful boards are increasingly focused on a broad range of stakeholder interests, including environmental and social impacts.

Chapter 4

BOARD UNDERPERFORMANCE

The most obvious boardroom problems are people related. Anybody who has sat on or reported to a board has some experience of these people-centric challenges. When joining any board, it's crucial for all potential members to check their egos at the door and be crystal clear on their motives. The key questions, of course, are whether they add value, and whether the organisation is a good fit for them and vice versa.

Korn Ferry, the world's largest executive recruiting firm, recently prepared a report on boardroom mechanics in which they noted a number of problematic characters that make regular appearances on the boardroom scene. There are the egocentrics, who need to make everything about themselves; the hand-grenade throwers, who are unnecessarily argumentative; the captives of compliance, who focus exclusively on the rules (rooting the board in one spot); the hobbyhorse jockeys, who always pull the conversation towards their favourite topic (usually their area of expertise); the non-stop talkers, who waste everybody's time with longwinded and unnecessary monologues; and, finally, the in-over-their-heads directors, who constantly display their lack of expertise and preparation.[13]

An important aspect of director-performance management is the regular provision of feedback, providing opportunities for questions, advice, and direct observations of the director at the boardroom table. Peer evaluations are a great way for directors to assess each other, and chair feedback to each director is crucial.

The critical factor is engaging the underperforming director in a process to improve their performance and, consequently, that of the entire board,[14] for example, professional development in a specific skill set, or capacity building in a particular area, mentoring, or organisational psychologists for behavioural issues.[15]

Underperforming directors can be liabilities for boards, and the chair's role is to provide support to get those directors where they need to be or let them go. Individual directors and the board as a whole should be reviewed annually. This can be facilitated externally or by the independent chair.

A recent high-profile example of perceived board underperformance was called out in the New South Wales Royal Commission into the affairs at Crown Casino, with a view to assessing the fitness of the casino to continue to hold a licence, without which their business model would be largely decimated. The outcome of this enquiry brought home the extreme nature of the consequences that can flow from faulty stewardship and inadequate visibility for boards. Boards must 'not lose sight of the need for transparency and, perhaps most importantly, the ability to build a culture of collective problem-solving between management and board'.[16]

I recognised the owner's frustration with his board in one of my earliest board-role interviews. The owner, Dino Strano (Winslow Constructors), told me he had sacked all of the previous board members. They were, he said, not 'committed to the priority of driving my business' so he had shown them the door.

I was very sceptical of Dino's story until he told me about his family. He had built a successful civil engineering business from scratch, having started his career on the tools himself. He had a wonderful, close family, with three bright kids, all of whom would one day join the business. There was absolute clarity in Dino's vision for the business. It was to be an intergenerational business, built on foundations of family values, trust and integrity. It was the clarity of this vision that resonated with me. I likened it to my own father's ambitions for Givoni Mills.

Even the once-bitten-twice-shy CEO Trevor kept the board at arm's length initially. Reporting to the previous board had been like walking in a minefield, and Trevor wasn't going to trust the new group until we could prove that things were going to be different.

I was determined to earn the trust of Dino and Trevor through persistence and effort. I tried to demonstrate that I was genuinely interested in improving the business (which was true) by steering conversations away from day-to-day matters and towards macroeconomic and broader-business-model issues. This meant pushing for information that could inform longer-term strategic decisions, and being totally focused on robust discussions on the topics that really mattered to Dino and Trevor.

What were the issues that kept them up at night? That's what we thrashed out in the boardroom. The board papers created a backdrop only; there were only three or four things that truly impacted their business prospects at any given time, and that's what we discussed in board meetings. I told Trevor I wasn't going anywhere, and he was not going anywhere either. Seven years later we are all still here, working together better than ever. Everyone has a role to play. At Winslow, the whole was great than the individual parts, and I'm proud that the board I chair has a key role to play now and into the future.

REGULATING THE BEHAVIOUR OF BOARDS

There is a reason this book doesn't have the word 'governance' in the title (although it does refer to it quite a bit). Governance can be a problem in and of itself. Boards are of course governed by rules—lots of them. *The Corporations Act* is clear that the board should be a deliberative corporate governance body. By law, directors are there to make key decisions about the company's direction, and to provide crucial executive oversight. A key skill that enables directors to make sound decisions on material issues is, of course, risk management. One of the board's chief duties is to keep the organisation from throwing itself headlong into risky waters that could swallow the company, its staff and its shareholders.

When there is an abject failure in exercising a duty of care, and/or reckless behaviour that can be traced back to the board, that board can and should be held accountable. The corporate veil—the gauze that separates the company from those running that company—may be extremely difficult to pierce, but when it is, the consequences can fall on the board members like a tonne of bricks.

There is no end to new legislation for boards to ponder, be it modern-slavery bribery, whistleblower legislation, bullying and harassment legislation, industrial manslaughter, or privacy and cyber laws. For directors, it's as though the boardroom is constantly under siege from legislators. Story after story appears in the daily press about poorly behaving boards that are either perceived to be asleep at the wheel or at odds with changing community standards. There has been a proliferation of class actions against the boards of listed companies, often related to a failure to comply with continuous disclosure obligations; royal commissions tearing apart the reputations of Australian banks; and the directors of a casino falling on their swords in the wake of failures of corporate governance.

Harder still for the reputations of individual directors on boards is the emergence of new legislation—workplace health and safety, taxation, environment, privacy—that threaten to pierce the corporate veil and hold directors personally accountable for their actions or inactions. Hence directors' and officers' insurance premiums have been skyrocketing in recent times.

The recent introduction of industrial-manslaughter laws, which can hold directors personally responsible should there be a systemic breakdown in safety processes, has alarmed and divided opinion on how far one can hold directors responsible for the mistakes of others (typically management).

The Whistleblower Act was another initiative aimed at addressing poor behaviour within organisations, enabling people—employees usually, but also other stakeholders such as contractors, customers or suppliers—to bypass the CEO and go straight to the board and trigger internal investigations anonymously. This process captures bullying, sexual harassment, and fraudulent behaviour, which destroys organisational culture and is clearly at odds with societal standards and expectations.

The consequence for boards around Australia, weighed down by this emerging legislation that is seemingly focused on regulating leadership behaviour, is a trend towards risk aversion. Non-executive directors in self-preservation mode can end up more concerned about personal reputation than their real priorities, which involve driving shareholder value. A risk-averse culture at board level is an unmitigated disaster for a mid-market private business, let alone a small cap-listed firm.

The corporate veil was once made of stiffer and thicker stuff than it is today. Over the last few decades, there have been increasingly difficult-to-ignore calls for directors' heads on spikes. These calls for increased accountability are entirely reasonable. This accountability is universally accepted as necessary for the protection of staff and creditors, where boards allow a business to continue to trade beyond the period where that business is solvent; the proof evidenced in a going-concern test, which shows whether a company can pay its debts as and when they fall due. This can be easy to say, but difficult to measure.

In 2015 at ASX-listed company, BSA Limited, we had a major contractual dispute on a construction site, which meant we were not being paid for our work although we still had an ongoing obligation to complete the job and pay our staff and subcontractors. The cash drain was choking the company. The walls were caving in around us as we breached our banking covenants with the bank. However, the credit team was supportive (the unfortunate term is 'bad bank') and the tactic we took was to appoint our own independent reviewer to build a recovery plan, acting as if we were in voluntary administration but without pressing this button.

We shared this recovery plan with the bank, and basically it was in their hands as to whether or not the company survived. They gave us the green light, and we delivered on the plan to the letter. In situations like this, the easy decision is to hand over the keys for fear of legal repercussions and to protect one's own brand. The braver decision is to tough it out, individually as a chair and collectively as a board. Unity at board level and collective resolve around the table is tested in times of adversity, more so than when things are going smoothly.

As long as directors act ethically, in good faith, and with a commensurate level of care and concern, the corporate veil will continue to offer protection in the form of the business-judgement rule. The rule gives businesses and the boards that govern them a wide berth in terms of the commercial risks that organisations must take. Honest mistakes can and should be forgiven. Some risks, even catastrophes, are simply unforeseeable. Effective risk management doesn't need to prepare for every eventuality. If the board wrings its hands endlessly about the what-ifs, it will not be able to fulfil its higher entrepreneurial function of navigating growth and creating shareholder value.

Though the board might not have a crystal ball that provides a clear picture of the future, it should be possible to imagine the consequences of, for example, a major supply-chain disruption, a recall, or a catastrophic IT or equipment failure on your ability to continue functioning. 'We didn't see this one coming', often accompanied by a dismissive shrug of the shoulders, doesn't exactly inspire confidence in customers, employees or shareholders. Instead it demonstrates a failure of board leadership.

The same is true for business risks. The board can and should be held responsible if it rushes the company headlong into irresponsible commercial deals. This doesn't mean the board should endlessly weigh—or, for that matter, avoid—risk. A key component of the entrepreneurial spirit is risk appetite, and a good board should, if anything, tip the organisation towards rather than away from risk. High-performing boards aren't gluttons for risk, but they're not shrinking violets either. Directors' and officers' insurance should be put in place as a backup. Assuming the board isn't engaging in criminal behaviour, the insurance will cover the directors in most instances.

It's the board's job to provide a clear vision and insight into strategy that management can then execute. The board provides oversight; it doesn't overreach. While it's true that boards can take too many risks, some boards nowadays take far too few. Ignore risks, and sooner or later the board and the business will run aground.

POISONOUS POLITICS

Nothing makes board meetings more tedious and unproductive than politics; that is, when directors have a bone to pick with other members of the board, or when directors have an agenda that is entirely separate from what the board is trying to accomplish collectively. Meetings can quickly become side-tracked. Rather than focusing on strategy and vision, the board can get bogged down in long-simmering feuds, and people can be at cross-purposes with each other.

The worst example of this is activist shareholders who want to appoint their own representative to the board under a keep-everyone-honest brief. Manoeuvring and elbowing for position simply have no place in the boardroom, and experienced chairs recognise this from the outset.

The more that politics exists around the boardroom table, the more directors will turn their focus inward, discussing internal issues and missing important opportunities to grow the business. Rather than building shareholder value, the infighting will be eroding it day by day. As with so much else, a high-functioning board is a product of attitude. Everybody who takes on the role of director or chair (and especially the latter) needs to bring a sense of gravity to the task. Debate should be robust and serious, with a tangible pull towards consensus. If agreement is impossible, determine what is standing in the way of consensus. Is the issue a difference of opinion, or is it a personality conflict? If it's the latter, reset and take another run at it, using a set of agreed-upon facts. Enquiry should be non-threatening, and there should be a distinct aura of trust and cooperation for the good of the asset under management.

A board role is not for everyone. Collective decision-making can be extremely frustrating for some. Business is challenging enough without conflict and tension in the boardroom.

As chair, I have sometimes asked board members to retire, especially once I have sensed frustration and tension in the room. I can live with and encourage the black-hat inquisitor, but I have zero tolerance for the angry-ant-style director who gets personal in attacking management, and/or creates an atmosphere of tension and fear.

Being part of a board should be about living in and coping with ambiguity. There is never perfect information, and never a right or wrong answer, just an optimal decision; the CEO is persuading one way, but there are other courses of action. In certain situations the board might back the management team in handling a situation, even if the path is not certain. The board's role is to support and offer feedback, and to try to make a better decision.

Directors should be people who can cope with this. A chair might need to have a couple of conversations outside the boardroom to determine the resilience and grit of potential directors. If there are existing abstainers or dissenters, this is a sure sign of problems that need to be dealt with.

'This very public saga [for Crown] has served as a firm reminder to all organisations that effective risk management and key corporate governance principles must rise above any personality-based issues, that quick action is needed when the warning signs become evident, and transparency and good culture are not negotiable...'[17]

BOARDS AS EXCLUSIVE CLUBS

Some boards simply go through the motions. A less than lofty ambition of protecting shareholders from management inadequacies is not a *raison d'etre*. The media constantly portrays and exposes boards that behave badly. This antiquated model of leadership, where boards are led by self-important captains of industry, leads to exposure and anger in the broader community, and a perception of exclusivity where confirmation bias self-perpetuates.

As a young man I was in awe of boards, and particularly the chair at the helm. I'm not really sure why. I just saw the chair as the pinnacle of a successful business career. Who wouldn't want such a role? When I was a young solicitor working at a Collins Street law firm, senior partners of the firm and/or clients would invite me to the Savage or Athenaeum Club for lunch. Since I was also a downtrodden Demons AFL supporter, an invitation to the Melbourne Cricket Club members' dining room was something to savour. I never really fitted in, however, or felt comfortable. A son of a clothing manufacturer, with Jewish heritage and Eastern European blood made me somewhat self-conscious.

It was a quandary. I coveted a successful legal and business career, and there was no room in the Givoni family business anyway, with four of my brothers already ensconced there. Also, my father had strongly encouraged me to take this different path. I wanted to fit in, but I was made to feel different. To be truthful, I was a bit different, and that was the problem: 'different' didn't really work for 'club' membership induction.

I hated wearing a suit and tie. It was the tie that ruined my morning. Brian Blythe, chair at Spotless, always had a morning greeting for me in the car park: 'Come and see me when you're dressed,' he would say, referring to the tie hidden in my suit pocket and the suit jacket hanging over my right shoulder. I loved Brian as a mentor, and understood the theory that if you didn't look the part, you couldn't be the part.

I recall one board meeting where one of the members called me his 'Jewish Rottweiler'. It was his way of making sure I wasn't too comfortable, that I should stay in my box and chew on the next bone. These early experiences shaped my attitudes and steered me towards encouraging leadership from all walks of life.

There is no room on a board for hubris, only humility. A board is a team, and a business is an even larger team. And, using a famous football line, a champion team is always better than a team of champions. Diversity of gender, race, experience, disability and sexuality all contribute to an inclusive culture that allows curious questions to be asked, and courageous conversations to take place. This leads to a culture where the team can focus on the creation of value.

The tradition of boards as exclusive clubs has effectively alienated a majority of the population from entering business at that level. Gender is perhaps the primary catalyst for moving an organisation towards a more diverse and inclusive culture.

Telstra's appointment in 2021 of entrepreneur Bridget Loudon is to be commended. Loudon, aged thirty-three, is the founder of online employment marketplace, Expert360. Also commendable is the appointment of renowned academic and former Intel executive Genevieve Bell at the Commonwealth Bank, but these two examples are still very much the exception rather than the rule.[18]

BOARDS BY THE BOOK

A board that is run by the book is usually the result of a board chair that has in mind what boards *should* do, not what they *can* do. They know the board should provide a legally compliant framework and management oversight. They know it should create some separation between ownership and management. They stack the board with those well versed in compliance (often lawyers and accountants), and then hope for the best.

More often than not, the result is a stolid and conservative board that is far too compliant, if there is such a thing. The board fulfils the purpose for which it is established, but nothing more than this. Boards by the books are too concerned with lowering risk, too interested in self-protection. They protect the asset rather than growing it.

If the chair of the board has a compliance-first mindset, it's perfectly natural to fill the boardroom with those who have extensive knowledge of compliance issues and the legislative framework. Compliance-first chairs pack their boardrooms with pencil pushers. These boards lead fully compliant organisations that are tucked in around the corners as tightly as a drill sergeant's bed, but these same boards have very little to offer in the way of entrepreneurial leadership.

BLOATED BOARDS

Generally, the more people involved in decision-making, the harder it is to reach consensus. As a result, I advocate for smaller rather than larger boards. Think about the last time you chose a place to eat. If there were two of you, it might have been the work of a moment. If there were three or four of you, there might have been a few discarded options. Now let's say a dozen of you are heading out for lunch. If you try to find a place that makes everybody happy, it'll be dinnertime before you've reached a decision. Just because a board table has ten seats, it doesn't mean every one of them needs to be filled.

There comes a point when adding more and more directors has diminishing returns. High-functioning boards are no larger than they have to be. They are streamlined and nimble decision-making bodies, never bloated immovable objects. Bloated boards are often an outcropping of the board-by-the-books mentality.

Generally, the larger the board, the more conservative it becomes. It hems and haws when presented with opportunities, but it finds consensus quickly when it comes to managing risk or assuring compliance. This type of board puts out fires rather than setting them and then harnessing the heat and energy those fires produce.

Keep the table small, and make sure that everybody around it has elbowroom. A board of eight members might sound reasonable, but when reporting executives are included, it adds up to a lot of people in the room. The ideal number for an inaugural board for a medium-sized company is probably a chair plus three or four directors. A chair, founder, non-executive director, CEO and CFO (five members) is a perfect start for a mid-market private-company board.

There is some debate about whether a board should have an odd or even number of members; however, with the chair as the casting vote there'll never be an actual deadlock, even if there are equal numbers on both sides of a proposal. Odd numbers will make arriving at a decision a little easier, but it's sometimes better to even the scales so there's a stronger need for consensus before the chair casts their vote.

LACK OF SUCCESSION PLANNING

The relationship between the chair and CEO is sacrosanct and critical to the success of any business. It is part of the chair's priority tasks to mentor, support and hold accountable the CEO for delivery on management forecasts. It's a close relationship with just a tinge of tension.

Changes required at C-suite level should never catch the board napping. When a departure is imminent, there should be a suitable candidate waiting in the wings. Recruiting from outside, especially at CEO level, is fraught with risk. Succession from within is the preferred path. At the very least, there should be a short list of viable internal candidates. Succession planning is never more important than when the board is trying to push the organisation off its plateau and onto a steep uphill climb.

Without a succession plan, there may be a leadership vacuum. It can be an interesting challenge to convince a founder that it's time for them to step back from the CEO role, but it's especially important if the company aims to be an attractive asset for potential buyers. Barring a steady hand on the tiller, investors or buyers want to see a smooth transition from founder to professional executive that is bankable.

When appropriate notice is given, succession planning should include looking both inside and outside the organisation for a best fit for the role. It seems that the larger the company, the more likely it is that it will look at outsiders to fill that crucial corner office; however, the best candidate might be just down the hall.

A key task for the chair is to ensure that the CEO annually produces a talent map that shows depth within management ranks; 360-degree evaluations can also be helpful, if done well.

The outcome must be allocation of training dollars to tailored management development, with particular focus on those who report directly to the CEO.

Mapping talent means avoiding bias and subjectivity, a difficult task indeed. I am a huge advocate of thinking outside the obvious when assessing talent. I owe much of my career to this sort of thinking. When I applied for a job after making the decision to change careers, a wonderful, thoughtful man called Brendon O'Brien gave me my first executive role. I wanted out of law and into the commercial world. I had no contacts and answered an advertisement in the newspaper. Brendan was honest at the interview and told me that in a shortlist of two, I was the dark horse; a risk, compared to the safe bet. Yet he took the punt, and I will be forever grateful. Nowadays I consistently do the same thing, and advocate perspiration over inspiration almost every time.

Succession planning should extend to the board members as well. Board refresh is healthy. Tenure should be evaluated periodically. Board appointments should also be staggered so there is a combination of both fresh approach and corporate memory on the board. There is a lot of value in corporate memory, and to change the dynamic does not necessarily bring added worth.

Although there is a need to refresh and revive, much will depend on the individual and their circumstances, and the needs of the business. There shouldn't be a set period of time for a person to be on the board; if the board is working well, there is no need to set a time limit. There should always be awareness of successorship at the management and board level. If it's a highly successful board and leadership team, it should be left alone.

Directors should be self-aware and honest with themselves when it comes to evaluating members of the board. They should recognise when there is a change in the air, and be alert to a market dynamic that means certain members may no longer be suitable for the board. They might not be the right fit in terms of culture, or have the best interests of the company in mind anymore; in short, they may not be a leader the business and its employees can respond to.

KEY TAKEAWAYS

✓   A successful board builds a high-performance team.

✓   Great boards build a culture of collective problem-solving between management and board.

✓   Boards are a team; egos should be left at the door,

✓   The chair plays a crucial role in ensuring diversity of opinion, and facilitating consensus though healthy, respectful debate.

✓   The chair should be alert to early warning signs of dysfunction at the boardroom level, and have zero tolerance for undermining attitudes and behaviour.

✓   The ideal initial number of directors on a private, mid-market board is five, including the CEO and CFO.

✓   An effective board will always be proactive in succession planning for management and the CEO in particular, as well as for the board members themselves.

✓   Boards have an important role in mentoring and guiding the CEO while holding the CEO accountable for management forecasts.

Chapter 5
GETTING STARTED

Choosing a board isn't something we *let* happen; it's something we *make* happen. This means thinking carefully about what a board will do for the company, and the kind of people who will sit on it.

Kick-off meetings with owners are paramount when choosing an appropriate board. If there's an exit in mind, in either the short or mid term, the directors should be adept at shaping the business for the next owner. This is very different to a situation where the objectives are intergenerational, in which case it would be more about being the bridge of continuity in order to seamlessly transition from the founder to the logical successor within the broader family. The objectives for each are vastly different, and so are the skills and sensitivities required around the board table.

Beyond the owner's objectives established at kick-off meetings, there should be a gap analysis, and then a strategy plan (of sorts) that navigates towards the end objectives while addressing the gaps identified early on; that is, a blueprint that looks beyond the annual budget cycle to an assessment of the material considerations shareholders and other stakeholders value.

Rather than adhering dogmatically to a particular strategy, high-functioning boards continually revise their plans to adapt to the on-the-ground reality. In many industries, things change far too quickly to make and keep plans. They give the company much-needed agility (a key component of the success of B.O.A.R.D.S.).

Of course, a business plan is essential, which should include a 12-month operating budget and a larger-window strategic plan, usually in the range of three to five years. However, plans only go so far. People change, the environment changes, and the competition changes rapidly. We have all seen companies start to lose track of their plans, which become historical reports far too quickly, rather than living breathing documents.

Longer-term planning skills should be among the first things considered when developing or refreshing a board. This should be led by the chair, and begin before the board is finalised so fit-for-purpose directors can be recruited. If the board chair and owners are aligned on the longer-term objectives, and the macro factors that can and will impact these, the framework is sound.

The CEO can focus on the here and now, but the board and owner representatives must use the precious time they have together at board meetings to continually refer to the longer-term key objectives, and determine whether or not they are still on track. Too often a board can get dragged back into operational details for which it can add only minimal value. The board should get out of the way of management, and elevate discussions to the broad strategic themes at all times.

Whatever the reason you established the company, and whatever the reason you continue in a leadership role in the company, a high-functioning board will help you achieve your objectives. If you want to be the largest company in your niche, the nimblest organisation in your space, a board can help you do that. Capture and document your expectations, and when you're interviewing for board seats, discuss these expectations and objectives frankly with the candidates; articulating your objectives means you'll be one step closer to achieving them.

THE ROLE OF THE CHAIR

If we were to make analogous board roles to those of a music band, the chair would be the lead singer. Without a strong lead singer, the band wouldn't have much hope of achieving commercial success. Avoid the trap of appointing a high-profile 'lead singer', a well-known and recognised name. It's not about profile or having a grand public persona. That's just ego for ego's sake.

The best lead singers care little for the rock-and-roll lifestyle or the other trappings of success. They take their art seriously, bringing a sense of humility and gravity to their task. They take the behavioural lead, making sure that band meetings never become long boozy lunches. They see the work they do as incredibly important, and they don't hesitate to pull up their band mates when they've had a bad outing. The lead singer has confidence—enough confidence to seize opportunities, but not so much that they leap without looking. They're the calm, steady hand on the wheel.

When the lead singer stands in the spotlight at the front of the stage and hits the right note, taking the audience into the palm of their hand, an electric current of confidence flows through the rest of the band. Following the lead singer's lead, the other members of the band will put in, night after night, the best performances of their careers.

An ideal chair is a bruised all-rounder, someone who has been in a number of different careers and roles throughout the earlier stages of their career.

A good chair empathises, not just with the other people in the room but also with those who report to the board. As chair, I lean on my experience in previous roles. I've been a lawyer, general counsel, head of strategy, head of sales and marketing, head of acquisitions and divestments, general manager of operations, and company secretary, and I've filled a number of corporate finance roles. I understand the different languages of those roles, and I also understand what it's like to sit in the office day in and day out. I know what is reasonable to expect from members of management, and what is unreasonable. I know when they're prevaricating, and I know when they're giving it to me straight. I can earn their respect and complete honesty by showing that I have experience in the technical elements that inform their reporting.

Just as with a band, having the wrong leader in the boardroom can be extremely difficult to recover from. If the board is formally structured, however, sacking the chair can be extremely difficult. What's more, it's something of an admission of defeat. In summary, ensure there are no shortcuts in the process of making this first appointment, that of the chair.

These 'ten commandments' for business leaders, as Cunningham calls them, are what Buffett cites for his vast amount of board-room triumphs.[19]

Warren Buffett's ten commandments:

1. Selecting the right CEO comes before all other tasks.
2. You should discuss a CEO behind his/her back.
3. Act as if you work for a single absentee owner.
4. Be fair, swift and decisive
5. If you perceive a problem, speak up about it.
6. When no one is listening, reach out to the absentee owner: shareholders.
7. Sometimes a leader has to burp at the table.

8.   Don't let any outside consultant decide how much people get paid.
9.   There is only one way to avoid audit issues: pry.
10.   When it comes time to choose your own replacement, refer to commandments 1 through 9.

My most hated task is removing a CEO, but it's part of the chairman's role. Sometimes it's best to think of it as doing both sides a favour. In my experience, if regular feedback is being provided, and key deliverables are clear, the ultimate exit of the CEO has a sense of inevitability to it.

THE CHAIR AND THE OWNER

For the board to do all that it can and should do, owners need to cede some level of control. It's common for high-functioning boards to include the owners as directors, but an owner should not be the chair, and ultimately not even the CEO. The best boards act as a bridge between ownership and management, and when there is an owner standing on both sides of the bridge, and sometimes in the middle as well, the board is essentially powerless; it becomes a structure without purpose. Unless the owner is willing to cede some control by handing over operations to a capable executive, and allowing carefully selected board members to speak on their behalf, the board exists, at best, in an advisory capacity only.[20]

In the simplest model, ownership sits above the board, but this belies the more complex back and forth that can occur in high-functioning boards. The major shareholders have the final say on the company's objectives, but a high-functioning board plays an important role in helping the owners decide what those objectives should be. Owners who get the most out of their boards are open to the advice that comes to them in this way and are prepared to let go.

The best owners I have worked with—those who have got the most out of their boards and me as chair or director—have recognised the importance of a strong relationship between the owner and the chair. These owners continually work with the chair, discussing progress and objectives. Some objectives are set in stone, while others are more flexible, adjusting to the realities of the moment. As these objectives change, frequent conversations between the owner and the chair can empower the chair to go to the other directors with a clear agenda straight from the horse's mouth. They will know exactly what the owner wants and why they want it, and they'll be able to guide the board towards the right decision in the moment.

Brandon Chizik, founder and CEO of RSEA, is an example of someone who puts well-placed trust in others. When I joined his board in 2015, at the invitation of his junior business partner, Sally, I walked into a totally dysfunctional room of directors. His PE partners, Champ Ventures, had two directors, with Brandon and Sally making up the board. I was the first independent non-executive director (NED).

The tension was palpable. Champ had recently bought in with a deal structure that Brandon regretted having agreed to. Earnings were stagnating, if not in outright decline. As founder and CEO, Brandon was not happy. Everything seemed to be a total mess. We eventually sorted it, but it took a number of chess moves to solve this puzzle.

Champ Ventures needed to back Brandon fully. Brandon was the heart and soul of the business, and we knew that once he felt supported, business morale would lift. We over-recruited and brought in talent that could take us well into the future. Terry, the new general manager, and Macca, CFO, were key appointments. Some key business-model decisions were made. Instead of being a reseller of other well-known brands, Brandon and the team developed their own safety-clothing brand, with a younger, more fashionable look and feel. The store footprint flourished, growing from twenty to sixty stores in five years. Social and digital media platforms were embraced.

The business eventually undertook a leveraged buy-out with ICG, an extremely supportive partner that has provided facilities for the net level of growth. Brandon and the management team now have majority control of the business. It's a new executive team. Part of my role as chair was to explain to Brandon that his previous executive team was not up to the task. It wasn't up to the challenge of running a larger business. We replaced the team with people who had come from larger businesses, with the track records to expand ranges, build teams, and deploy digital and social media strategies. That de-risked execution of the growth plans for all stakeholders.

Relationships don't have to be formal or developed in Collins Street (Melbourne) or George Street (Sydney) exclusive men's clubs. A conversation during a walk in the park or over a leisurely coffee can often be just as productive and illuminating as a conversation held between owner and chair with a desk between them. However you meet, bring an open mind to these conversations. Allow them to develop naturally. Be open and encourage openness in others. Not every idea that gets shared will be raised in the boardroom, but every conversation will help you and your chair better understand each other and your objectives.

Returning to the band analogy, the band manager (the owner) is the one who puts the band together. There's a lot of available talent, but putting a successful band together takes more than talent. Individual success and board success are only tangentially related. As in the music industry, there are plenty of talented solo performers out there. The solo performers can excel in executive roles, distinguishing themselves and doing credit to their employers; excellent board members, however, are a different breed.

Often, those who manage bands were once performers themselves, with successful solo careers. With that background, they might be tempted to step onto the stage and take hold of the microphone, or sling a guitar over their shoulder. In most cases, this would be a mistake. The best managers watch from the wings. They understand that making a hit song is a collaborative process; they know that if they were to take centre stage the band would take all their cues from them. It would stop being collaborative and start being dictatorial. It's far better for the manager to tell the members of the band what kind of music they want to hear and then let the band work together to produce something that fits those objectives.

The managers who get the most out of their bands are the ones who use them to do more than they could ever do on their own, or even as a member of the band. They allow the band to take them in new and interesting directions that might not have been considered by a solo act. The final decision about what gets released and what doesn't remains in the manager's hands, but they allow the talent they have put together to do the hit-making work unimpeded.

THE CHAIR AND THE CEO

One of the board's primary roles is to oversee execution by management of short- and mid-term business objectives. It measures CEO and executive-team performance against pre-agreed targets that are normally established collaboratively at annual budget-planning days.

A key relationship of mutual respect and trust must exist between the chair and the CEO. The CEO is directly responsible to the board. The chair effectively has a responsibility to oversee the performance of the business through the lens of the CEO, and ultimately to hold the CEO accountable on behalf of the ownership/founder group.

On boards that I chair, the CEOs and I talk often. I share with these CEOs my thought processes surrounding problems, and I encourage them to share any pertinent news. On the best boards, these relationships are based on good faith. The CEO and the chair don't have to be friends, but they should definitely be on friendly terms. They should be able to have frank and open conversations about the matters before the board. For as long as I have faith in the CEO and the job they're doing, I make sure to communicate this to the board. I've found that when the CEO knows they have the support of the board—whether or not the board receives good or bad news—they are more open in their reporting, and often better in their decision-making as well. Ron Evans, a great leader of AFL-presidency fame I once reported to, had a great saying: 'Give me good news early, but bad news even earlier.'

If other members on the board want to lay a particular problem at the feet of the CEO, the chair needs to filter and/or pre-assess these reservations. A key leadership role for the chair is to ensure the board speaks with one voice externally, including when it speaks to the CEO.

Ideally, executives report to high-functioning boards rather than sit on these boards themselves as formal members. The CEO, CFO and COO, and other reporting executives, will make an appearance at most board meetings, but they're there primarily to provide the board with data, insights and trends. The boardroom should be a safe place for open and transparent sharing of critical information. Elizabeth Hammack, author of *The Private Company Board of Directors Book*, offers the following helpful reminder, returning to it frequently in her book: 'Noses in, fingers out.'

The board should be aware of absolutely everything that is in its interest, but it should not meddle. Oversight and guidance should not cross the line into management itself. Crucially, this does not mean adopting a laissez faire attitude towards executive oversight. Noses should be in—*way* in. Fingers are in the pie when the board is doing something that should be properly left to management to do, but not when the board monitors and provides feedback to management about their performance in relation to pre-established goals jointly signed up to with the board at budget time.

Keeping the founder spirit means maintaining equilibrium between *taut* and *energetic*. Before introducing the oversight of a board, organisations are often like a slack rope. At one end of the rope there is a loose governance structure; at the other end there is an energised entrepreneurial spirit. The board picks up that rope and pulls on both ends, providing a tight and disciplined structure while simultaneously reinvigorating the founders' entrepreneurial energy.

Those who find leading a board incredibly rewarding are the ones who are able to maintain balance between the corporate and entrepreneurial world. They are able to take what they like from corporate structures without sacrificing the entrepreneurial verve that drove sustained growth in the first place.

I joined UHG, founded by entrepreneur Dr Brandon Carp, in the early stages of Brandon's entrepreneurial journey, when he took over a medical practice from his father and extended its offering to a business-outsource-processing company. Through smart enabling technology, UHG connected users such as insurance companies or law firms with the medical fraternity, addressing needs such as a collation of medical histories and independent medical reports.

Brandon and I were a small intimate board of two for many years. The board table was a coffee shop in South Yarra. Later, the board was extended to include Brandon's extremely talented lawyer wife, Nicky, and the first of two external CEOs and CFOs. We took a 16-year journey together through the founder phase. As we workshopped Brandon's objectives, a staged exit to private equity was the logical next step to further accelerate investment in technology, and fast-track growth.

The smart decisions were made around the board table: build stronger internal controls, introduce external auditors, and bolster the profile and big end of town experience. Andrew Basset, of Seek fame, and the recently retired Telstra CEO,

David Thodey, joined the board. While still nimble, UHG had the look and feel of a business on the cusp of corporatisation, and was more likely to attract PE investment with those pieces of the puzzle already in place.

Another key success factor was demonstrable distancing of the founder, Brandon, from exerting influence over the day-to-day fortunes of the business. As CEO, Rob Farmer was a strong outsider now reporting to a high-functioning, independent board. The partial sale of UHG to Square Peg/FiveV took place thirteen years after my first coffee with Brandon. My job as chair was done.

It's natural for businesses, as they and their founders age, to grow increasingly conservative. Protecting what has been built can become a subconscious priority, thereby stunting the rate of growth. Other, nimbler entrants might be pushed back for a time, but sooner or later they will find a way to elbow their way in or leapfrog existing product design with more innovative offerings.

A business called First5Minutes suffered from this syndrome. It was first to market with a professional fire-and-emergency-services training offer, and was an early adopter of high-rise-building fire drills, with well-appointed evacuation diagrams. When the founders sold the business to a family office investor, I was asked to represent the latter on the board. This was a tough assignment because the culture was blokey, with an almost military style of operating. There was little or no innovation, and a passive-aggressive hierarchical culture. It took seven years to turn the business around, including two acquisitions and injections of new executive talent. The product offer changed fundamentally to a broader risk-management consultancy, selling risk-assessment tools, crisis management, business resilience plans, property-facade inspections, and remediation. It became a totally transformed offer.

The establishment of the First Five Group board (incorporating the original First5Minutes division) was the antidote to this moribund culture that had stunted any innovation or growth. Its priority was to return the business to its more exhilarating entrepreneurial phase, but with a dramatically increased scope. Access to capital, with the active encouragement and support of the Roberts family office, Galabay, meant opportunities that were once out of reach could now be tabled and considered.

BUILDING TRUST

Ideally, the primary task of a newly appointed chair is to build trust and respect with the founders/owners and the CEO. Sometimes this respect is presumed by virtue of the reputation the chair has brought to the table, but this trust and respect need to be earned. The chair might be the very first outsider let into the closely knitted business tent. It can take time for this trust to be established, and might need to evolve simultaneously with the advocating of some tough business decisions.

Take whatever time is needed to build the confidence of the founders. Start somewhere, anywhere. Monthly board meetings that begin suboptimally could be a significant improvement over what the owners/founders had previously. The key is to make the meetings enjoyable, market focused, growth oriented, and conducted in the language of an entrepreneur.

The newly appointed chair will set the tone. Often it is best to start with one outsider; avoid stacking the board with multiple appointees at the outset. Work with the founders, a trusted external accountant or solicitor, and one or two senior managers.

The new or refashioned board must be anything but predictable, anything but a passive listening environment. Hopefully the owners/founders will look forward to attending, enjoy the experience, and garnish value from constructive debate on topics that really matter.

Boards that merely march to the sound of the owners' drum tend to be stagnant, achieving little, if anything. If the board isn't playing a substantial role in the shaping of the organisation's forward-looking vision, board meetings will be just another talkfest. The best boards are vehicles for robust discussion on industry trends, and the longer-term opportunities and challenges facing the business. A board agenda that focuses on analysing last month's financial results or compliance issues will rapidly lose the attention of entrepreneurial high-growth business owners. Lose the owner, and you lose the board.

One of the first boards I sat on as chair was a family-owned business called Maltra Foods, run by a wonderful, warm family of first-generation Russian heritage. The founder, Greg, was a taxi driver initially, before he started the food-manufacturing concern making dry-powder products like drinking chocolate, cake mix, chai latte, and sport supplements. It had innovative plant and equipment, and was a real success story. The idea of bringing an outsider like me into the fold came from Stephen, their trusted accountant, after he identified an underlying issue that needed urgent resolution.

Greg's preference appeared to be to build an intergenerational business, and he had ushered both his sons, Roman and Jack, into key management roles in the company.

Greg bravely took one step back, allowing me to clear the air and start tackling key issues around role clarity and organisational design. The dilemma was solved through organisational redesign and role clarity. We separated the brothers' roles. Roman would run manufacturing, and Jack would lead sales and marketing. Two more external appointments were made: a financial controller and GM of operations.

With these two new executives attending board meetings, we were able to devise a 3-year growth plan. We set bold targets for building proprietary brands (Arcadia and Green Spoon) and determined which brands could be fifty percent of the product mix by sales volume, at the expense of being a pure contract manufacturer.

The dynamic around the board table evolved, and the behaviour became professional and business-like. Everyone had enough to do without tripping over the roles of others. With success came confidence. With confidence came trust and mutual respect.

BOARD COMPOSITION

To use the earlier analogy, putting together a board is a lot like assembling a music band. If the mixture is right, and if everybody gets on the same page and stays there, the band will make beautiful music together. If the mixture is wrong, the result will please nobody. Introduce even a single toxic member into the mix—somebody who is highly volatile, has attendance issues, or has a separate project that they will always put first—and the group will never gain any traction.

Many of those who build boards from scratch start by looking for the wrong kinds of people; they look for people who will do their bidding rather than people who are capable and energetic visionaries. Business throws punches from every direction, and directors must be able to absorb these blows and hold their nerve.

Experience means a great deal, but it's not everything. There are certainly exceptions to this assertion, but professionals—even professional directors—generally have a shelf life. It is also essential to ensure that the experience of those under consideration is relevant. A few of the boards I've sat on have featured status-symbol appointments. They might be politicians or business leaders, and they are placed on the board, often with a pronounced lack of process, to make the company look good by association. Remember that good boards don't concern themselves with these kinds of optics.

Is the person you're considering a good fit for the board and its objectives? Do they have the kind of knowledge and experience that can help you solve the problems you're facing, or are you hoping they will lift the profile of your company? If the latter, you may be creating a problematic dynamic in the boardroom, and ultimately getting far less than you paid for.

Lead guitarist (balanced visionary)

In a band, the lead guitarist is every bit as integral to the band's success as the singer. They are often the one responsible for providing the foundation (a nice set of chords or an ear-catching melody line) that inspires the lead singer to put pen to paper. The boardroom analogue is the director who brings with him a wide and fast-running entrepreneurial streak. This is your ideal person, an essential cog in a high-functioning board.

The best directors of this kind regularly test the boundaries. They challenge the status quo and think in grandiose terms. They're not really detail oriented, but they can focus on the small picture when the moment demands it. They throw everything at the wall and see what sticks. Many of them bring contemporary technology—digital and social media expertise—to the table, and they're often shrewd thinkers when it comes to marketing. They've got their feet firmly planted in the industry's past, but they're more interested in its future.

Excellent boards, like excellent bands, find a way to balance visionary optimism and grounding scepticism, daring and prudence. They push against boundaries, but not so hard that they break through into dangerous and uncharted territory. The prudence and scepticism you need at the head of the table and elsewhere in the room are products of at least a moderately complete understanding of the legislative framework in which you operate. Without this knowledge, which is usually a product of experience, the scale can tip too far towards risk. Daring and optimism can be jet fuel for organisations in a growth phase, but ambition must be tempered by sound judgement and a complex understanding of what is possible.

Drummer (establishes rhythm and keeps time)

The cornerstone of every great rhythm section is the drummer. If the music the band produces is to be radio friendly and commercially viable, it needs to have that strong backbeat in place. In the world of business, this means numbers, and the drummer is the board's numbers guru.

This highly financially literate director can assess budgets, and the reporting from the CEO and CFO, extremely quickly. They can help prepare the organisation for external audit and pave the way for the lodging of the company's accounts. They have the clearest picture of the organisation's solvency, so they'll be the first to say when something is not financially feasible or prudent, and they will be the last to jump on board when evaluating risk. They see the world in black and white, and no board is complete without somebody with this kind of grounded certainty.

The drummer is absolutely essential, but they should not be allowed to dominate the rest of the band. If the numbers person drowns out the rest of the board, there's a risk of setting too simple and predictable a rhythm. As in a good band, the numbers person should be at least open to matching their beat to what the rest of the band thinks is possible. Great drummers will help the band pick up the pace when appropriate, not forgetting that all the other band members need at least a basic understanding of that back beat, of financial literacy.

Bass guitarist (prudent sage)

No rhythm section is complete without a bass player, a prudent and experienced sage who will ask the crucial question: 'What about this?' This director is the thorn in the side of management, but the chair's best friend. The bass guitarist will ask the board hard questions about performance, of both the business and the people tasked with running it.

When the rest of the band drifts into improvisational territory, the bass player will pull them back into more conservative channels. When everybody gets whipped up and excited about a new idea, the bass guitarist will help the band focus on the more realistic picture. When facing something new, they will draw important comparisons between what is being proposed and what has been tried—and has failed—before.

At the same time, when given the opportunity to solo, the bass player will surprise everyone with their virtuosity and unique offerings.

Keyboards, strings, and horns
(new pieces as they become appropriate)

The best boards, and bands, start small, with new members being added to fill a particular need. This could be a human resources expert, or someone well versed in disruptive technology-based change. It could be someone who understands the community and its most pressing needs, or someone with expertise in foreign markets.

By now there are four or five board members and that's as many as required to run a private mid-market business.

KEY TAKEAWAYS

✓ Having an effective and fit-for-purpose chair is critical.

✓ A board doesn't just happen; a kick-off meeting with the owners sets the objectives.

✓ The establishment of trust between the owners and the chair is essential.

✓ A gap analysis sets the strategy for the shape of the board. Is this a business to be handed to the next generation, or is it to be structured for ultimate or staged exit? Stay focused on this objective.

✓ The chair establishes the board depending on the requirements of the owners' objectives. Board skills should support the execution of these longer-term objectives.

Chapter 6
ALIGNMENT

Owners should bring the same level of discipline to the search for board members as they do to the search for executives, with the strategic objectives of finding people who can complement the board, add to the management team, and add value to the CEO to achieve the organisational goals.

Carey, Charan and Useem suggest that the personal qualities to consider when selecting a board leader should include:

- Business leadership, including crisis leadership
- Respect for and confidence in other directors
- Collaborative and restrained style
- Personally bonded with other directors
- Comfortable with own skin and station in life
- Resilient
- Complete candour and expectation of the same in others[21]

Putting the talent around the table in a collegiate way will facilitate better decision-making. The closer the team members are in terms of shared values, the better discussions the group will have, and the better the quality of the decisions made.

A board always needs a detail-oriented person, a governance expert to catch anything that is missed, and it's also useful to have a black sheep in the boardroom. In terms of behavioural attributes, directors need to be: respectful; loathe to indulge in point scoring; comfortable in their own shoes; calm when things aren't going their way; and able to contribute to a room of safety when it comes to trust and transparency. Psychological safety, trust and respect, which are all derived from empathy, are essential.

Be extremely careful not to allow personal relationships to cloud your judgement when seeking board members. If somebody you've known and broken bread with for years looks like a good fit, by all means reach out. Don't, however, try to make a square peg fit into a round hole. If the person is anything less than a perfect fit, you might find yourself in an extremely awkward situation.

Our recommendation is to use professional search firms who specialise in appointing chairs and NEDs using a disciplined process that considers the skills and behavioural traits being sought in ideal candidates, and broadens the pool of potential candidates belonging to the founders' network. Throw into the mix those people recommended by friends, colleagues and family, but offer no favours. Only the very best and most suitable candidates should succeed on their individual merits.

You might look at ten candidates and interview a couple of them; those who make strong additions to your board will demonstrate their worth immediately. They will clearly have done their homework, and they'll focus on how they can add value. They'll have a long list of accomplishments, but they won't dwell on these. Instead, they'll want to spend their time discussing their vision for your business.

The best interviewees are those who don't seem eager to please or impress. They are interested, but it's clear that it can't be taken for granted that they will accept the position if it is offered to them. They are evaluating you as much as, if not more than, you are evaluating them. When there's a good match, the meeting will feel serendipitous. Time will disappear and you'll get pulled into an engaging and productive conversation. This is what you want to see at your board meetings, so it's an excellent sign.

Like a great band, an exceptional board is much more than the sum of its parts. Board success is not about filling the room with talented individuals. It's about the meeting of minds, about the board's ability to cohere around the organisation's issues and opportunities. It's a given that the members of your board will have corner-office experience, but the boardroom demands an entirely different skill set. As with all successful collaborations, the egos get left at the door.

COMPENSATION

Public companies publish information about the remuneration of their board members, but private companies generally do not make this information public. Since public companies are generally larger than private ones, this can create an inflated picture of how much directors should be paid. Below is an outline of the kind of salaries you should be prepared to pay your board members based on the size of your organisation.

ANNUAL PROFIT	ANNUAL CHAIR SALARY	ANNUAL DIRECTOR SALARY
$3–5 million	$50,000	$40,000
$5–15 million	$80,000	$60,000
$15–30 million	$100,000	$80,000
$30–100 million	$150,000	$90,000
$100+ million	$200,000	$100,000

Some companies also offer board members a chance to get some skin in the game. If you're planning to take the company public or sell it, this, on top of a fair annual retainer, can provide further incentive for either chair or directors to grow the asset under management. Being invested in the business will sharpen the focus on the overriding objective of growing shareholder value, as they are themselves shareholders, in total alignment with the founders. Incentives like this can help attract exceptional board members, so it's definitely something to consider.

In my experience, those private-company founders that do offer shares, or options, at fair value to both board members and senior management, are more likely to achieve the aligned behaviour that can extend the entrepreneurial spirit and continued growth trajectory of the business. Having an owner's mentality deep within the leadership ranks reinforces the founders' culture and shared values. Some founders may see this as a loss of control and something to fear, but my job as chair is to fight tooth and nail to disavow founders of this somewhat outdated view.

Board members can also be promised a percentage of the increase in value under their direction, often described as 'shadow equity' (realised when the company sells), or they can be offered ordinary shares at an attractive price, which will, if all goes well, be worth considerably more to the members when their tenure is up.

Some organisations offer an opportunity to purchase shares along with a helping hand in the form of a non-recourse company loan to cover most or all of the cost of the share purchase. I am not at all a believer of full-recourse loans as they can have perverse consequences. If, for example, the company's share price drops precipitously for any reason, a full-recourse loan can create behaviour that is suboptimal. A company never wants to be in the situation of tying people to the organisation for the wrong reasons.

I have seen directors and senior executives hold onto their positions well beyond their use-by date simply because they are in debt to the organisation. They don't want to leave and cut a cheque as they walk out the door. At Spotless, this was loosely referred to as a 'golden handcuff'. I was one of those senior executives at risk of having to pay back the loan shortfall when PEP privatised the business. I lawyered up and dodged this bullet, but it was hardly a dignified way to end a 15-year executive stint.

THE BOARD MEETING

Board meetings should be engaging sessions that bring collective focus onto the problems and opportunities that require deliberative decision-making, followed by concerted action. The key word here is *engaging*. Governance, compliance, risk management and processes cannot be ignored, but they should also not be allowed to dominate board meetings. Directors can find their enthusiasm waning quickly if they never get the opportunity to exercise their entrepreneurial abilities.

The board's focus will be kept sharp, and directors will be continually engaged, when the board is a vehicle for leadership. The board is a monitoring tool as well, but its primary focus should be on growing the asset under management. The board should have its hand on the rudder, not in the bowels of the ship plugging leaks. That can be left to the executives.

Independent directors who bring entrepreneurial verve to the table will want to tackle the larger questions about the company's vision and direction. Operational details and budget lines won't keep them interested. Check on important policies, but don't get bogged down in them.

The chair, with the backing of the owners, should clearly communicate to management what they will be expected to elevate to the board and what they will be expected to handle themselves. If, for instance, a whistleblower raises a serious complaint—perhaps a toxic culture problem, or concerns about corruption, or unfair hiring and firing practices—it should be elevated immediately. The board should discuss the issue at length and decide on an appropriate course of action. A complaint about an executive below the rank of CEO should be resolved in the corner offices unless there is a clear conflict that will cast doubt on the legitimacy of the executive decision.

To keep discussions or track, I draft board papers that focus on the big questions rather than the small ones. As chairman, I start each meeting by asking if there is anything not in the board papers that needs to be discussed. I close with something similar, making sure there are no outstanding issues that either haven't been covered or have been covered insufficiently.

A typical meeting might look at how the CEO is tracking operations against targets. The CEO might raise the issues that are keeping them up at night and propose a solution, or range of solutions, that the board can grind between its teeth. The board will spend some time analysing financial reports, often including a conversation with the CFO, and border environmental or social issues. There might also be discussions about safety and risks, and, depending on the needs of the moment, the board might also spend time looking at sales and marketing reports, major HR issues, and pending legal matters.

Even if all of this is covered, it doesn't mean the board had a high-quality meeting. If, for instance, a particular department is missing its targets by a wide margin, is under budget, or is otherwise underperforming, a good board conversation will move beyond a simple understanding of the issue and its causes. The board's focus should be on initiatives that will help the department get back on target, and ensuring that the board adds value beyond financials. Good meetings don't dwell on problems; they move quickly to solutions. They don't dwell on implementation—that is management's domain.

The most productive meetings run for about three to four hours. When meetings are scheduled for five or even six hours, the last few hours are rarely productive. At the other end of the scale, trying to cover everything in two hours will lead to rushed decisions and unfinished business. Rubber-stamp boards can wrap things up in an hour or two, but rarely accomplish anything.

Board meetings should take place at least monthly. They can be more frequent than this if there are regular issues that require the board's input, but meeting semi-weekly is usually more than is necessary and often creates the need to raise issues just to give the board something to do with its time. With more time between the meetings, you'll also be less likely to defer issues that need discussing, which just causes a backlog of unfinished business that must be addressed before turning to new matters.

If there is time, try to do a deep dive on one of the strategic planks at least once every few months. Whatever it is, it should be a key issue that needs more than a cursory examination. Try to push the matter much further than you would in the regular course of board meetings. This is a great opportunity to look in novel directions, and your 'lead guitar player' should be allowed to shine during these sessions.

Once annually, the board should meet to review not just the company's progress against its objectives, but also its own progress. It should also meet at the beginning of each year to discuss and plan for the year ahead. These sessions should be over and above the usual board meetings.

Emergency sessions should be convened when necessary, but only when the matter truly demands all hands on deck. If the matter is urgent, directors should be prepared to shuffle their schedules as necessary. This is the job.

Throughout the year, directors should keep detailed minutes of all board meetings. An informal atmosphere can lead to extremely productive idea-sharing sessions, but formal structures still need to be in place. All decisions, both discussed and made, need to be logged in the minutes. Keep detailed notes highlighting areas for further analysis and research.

Of course, the work of a director goes beyond meetings, and there is likely to be more work for directors as part of subcommittees. The most common subcommittees include the disciplines of audit, remuneration, and corporate development.

KEY TAKEAWAYS

✓ Selection and recruitment require professional support and a clear understanding of the skills matrix and needs.

✓ A board is a team, and directors need to be supportive, entrepreneurial, spirited team players.

✓ Curiosity, learning from experience, and applying the lessons learnt to different business situations are all important.

✓ Incentivisation of board and management can be an area of contention.

✓ Remuneration must be appropriate and aligned to longer-term objectives.

✓ Board meetings should be engaging and focus on consensual problem-solving.

✓ Transparent discussion should be minutes, followed by concerted action.

Chapter 7
BOARD ESSENTIALS TOOLS

While not an exhaustive list, this chapter itemises some of the essential tools that owners should expect to see established when introducing a highly effective board.

TOOL A: LEADERSHIP STRUCTURE

This tool establishes clarity in the roles of owner, board and management.

Owner:

- Sets expectations; has a crystalline long-term objective
- Let's go of day-to-day control
- Empowers board and appoints independent chair
- Receives regular updates

- Sets dividend policy
- Agrees on board charter
- Agrees with chair-appropriate delegations of authority
- Signs off on appropriate incentives
- Builds alignment at all levels

Management:

- Develops business plan
- Achieves annual financial targets
- Builds executive team around CEO and CFO
- Establishes appropriate culture, and behavioural standards
- Is empowered under delegation of authority to make operational decisions
- Reports to board on progress against plan

Board:

- Identifies and focuses on delivering owners' objectives
- Builds coherent strategic plan
- Ensures clear accountability between board and management
- Mentors, supports and monitors management performance
- Ensures successorship is in place at all levels
- Builds governance framework
- Is custodian of core values and expected behaviours; leads by example

TOOL B: BOARD CHAIR

An overview of the position description for the board chair:

RESPONSIBILITY	Minimum Performance Standard
LEADERSHIP OF BOARD	The board is an effective decision-making body that has earned the respect of key stakeholders, including, but not limited to, shareholders and management.
OWNERS' OBJECTIVES	The board understands key shareholder objectives and drives the board agenda towards achieving these.
BOARD MEMBERSHIP	Create a relevant and highly effective team. The board is to be a safe and trusting environment for management to report to.
CEO MENTORSHIP AND DIRECTION	Set priorities and closely monitor CEO performance. Provide feedback and support for the CEO, including setting appropriate key-performance indicators.
STRATEGY SETTING AND ANNUAL BUSINESS-PLAN APPROVAL	Ensure appropriate short- and mid-term planning is in place that is consistent with achieving overarching shareholder objectives.
SUCCESSORSHIP AND TALENT MAPPING	Talent management to be in place at both board and executive-team level.
DIVERSITY	The business leadership teams should be populated with skilled individuals from a range of diverse backgrounds.

COMPLIANCE	The board and executive team must put in place appropriate documented policies and training to comply with the regulatory environment in which the business operates.
SHAREHOLDERS' AGREEMENT AND COMPANY CONSTITUTION	Familiarity with these key framework documents is important to ensure the board carries out its duties in accordance with expectations.
REPORTING	Put in place reporting tools, including board reports, business plans and annual reports, as is appropriate for a business of this nature.
AUDIT AND ANNUAL GENERAL MEETING	Create a policy around the annual audit, publishing of accounts, declaration of dividends, and conduct of annual general meetings.
MEETING AGENDA, RECORD OF RESOLUTIONS, DELEGATIONS OF AUTHORITY	Put in place the necessary tools to ensure clarity as to where decision-making authority exists. Seek approval of this document, to be known as 'the delegations of authority'.
BOARD AND 360-DEGREE EVALUATIONS	Create an environment of honest and open feedback with regard to board and CEO performance.

Skills and experience for board chair

Background:

- Distinguished executive career, with focus on operational accountability
- Track record of successful leadership, and empathy for private and/or family-owned businesses
- Familiarity with boardroom dynamics

Skills:

- Deep operational knowledge and experience
- Strategic mindset
- Demonstrative evidence of growing and leading a comparable mid-market entrepreneurial business
- Mergers and acquisitions experience
- Excellent communication skills; has the ability to provide interpretation and advice in a clear, succinct manner

Behaviours:

- Gravitas
- High-level conflict-management capabilities
- Values team above self
- High emotional intelligence
- Bias to action
- Effective decision-maker

TOOL C: BUILDING A BOARD CHARTER

A charter is the rulebook or guide the board follows when determining how to conduct itself. A comprehensive board charter should address the following:

- Roles and responsibilities
- Role of the board
- Board composition
- Role of the chairman
- Role of individual directors
- Role of and delegation to the CEO
- Role of company secretary
- Term of office
- Board appointments
- Board processes
- Board meetings
- Director protocols
- Conflict of interest register
- Access to information and insurance
- Board evaluation
- Board director remuneration and expenses
- Director induction and development

TOOL D: BOARD-APPROVED POLICIES

These policies should address the following:

- Health and safety
- Environment

- Modern slavery
- Workplace violence, harassment and bullying
- Antidiscrimination/equal employment
- Diversity
- Privacy
- Anticorruption, compliance with anti-bribery laws
- Whistleblowing
- Antitrust/competition and fair trading
- Media and social media communications
- Document retention and record keeping
- Computer and internet

TOOL E: BOARD AGENDA AND CALENDAR

Example of a board agenda:

- Welcome and apologies
- Conflict of interest
- Minutes and actions from previous meeting
- Risk and safety review
- Items requiring approval
- Deep-dive topic of interest/presentation
- CEO update
- CFO update
- Review of strategy plan milestones
- Banking covenants
- General counsel summary of legal disputes register

Recommendations for developing an annual board calendar:

- Rotate venues
- Ideally, meeting held no later than third week after end of month
- Usually eight to ten meetings per annum
- Board papers to be distributed one week in advance
- Preferably board deck (PowerPoint or equivalent) no longer than sixty pages, including appendices
- One set of paginated papers only (no separate documents to be sent)
- One person responsible for minutes/actions and distribution of board papers, generally the company secretary (either CFO or general counsel)
- Standard agenda to be approved by the chair in advance
- Ideally, use technology for board approvals, e.g. DocuSign

Example of annual calendar of deep dives:

- February: Half-yearly financial review against business plan targets
- March: Strategy deep dive; report card against pre-agreed planning objectives
- April: Sales and marketing; review of pipeline, sales effectiveness and new-product offers
- May: People and talent management, discussion on succession planning
- June: Budget approval for next financial year

- July: Remuneration and bonus review; setting KPIs for new financial year from CEO down
- August: Risk-management framework review; focus on resources needed to manage priority risks effectively
- September: IT systems and cyber review
- October: Audit and accounts sign-off; safety deep dive
- November: Strategy reset (review of progress from March workshop each year)
- December: Year in review; results of board-evaluation tool

TOOL F: BOARD EVALUATION

This involves a constructive 360-degree or survey tool that provides feedback to the board chair and owners on how effectively the board is performing against pre-agreed objectives. Some indicators include:

- Effectiveness of board structure
- Strong leadership of the board by chairman
- Adequacy of meeting time without CEO
- Number and type of committees appropriate
- Productivity and efficiency of meetings
- Board papers received sufficiently in advance of meetings
- Adequacy of number of meetings
- Ensure average duration of meetings appropriate for purpose

- Board papers are relevant and address the issues to be considered
- Percentage of meeting time allocated to opposing views adequate
- Information system and data timely and accurate
- Information provided to board to assess projects adequate (both financial and non-financial)
- Number of hours spent on long-term strategic issues appropriate

Conclusion

Establishing a highly effective board should be a game changer. In a world environment where common sense is becoming less and less common, it ought to be the best decision a business owner ever makes. A board that is led by an independent chair and provides sound counsel allows owners to work *on* the business and not *in* it.

The establishment of a board will be a catalyst that signifies change. It can mean stepping up from founder-led entrepreneurialism to a necessary maturation of a business, leading to sustained growth, separate from the original founders' sole control.

The board can help owners crystallise goals and set razor-sharp objectives for their business. These objectives can range from retaining ownership and preparing for generational change on the one hand, to structuring the business for partial or total sale on the other. Once the owners' objectives have been established, the board, pursuant to its delegations of authority, has the mandate to execute.

Uncommon Sense has covered the essential methodology necessary to take all stakeholders on a journey towards establishing a highly effective board. In doing so, board members will create shareholder value, which, after all, is the primary reason for the board's existence.

Above all else, the chairman of the board should apply common sense and stay the course, with singular focus on the owners' objectives.

About the Author

MICHAEL GIVONI is a senior governance professional and non-executive director. He has acquired a portfolio of twenty directorships since 2010, across a diverse range of sectors, and has chaired corporations in construction, business services, training, digital automation, food manufacturing, and retail. Michael believes that the methodologies outlined in this book underpin board-effectiveness work across industries.

Michael has worked with ASX and SME companies with annual turnovers ranging from $20 million to $2.0 billion. He has been chair of boards that have overseen management teams of up to three thousand employees. His first direct experience with boards wasn't as a member but as a senior executive who reported to a board.

Before his time in management, he spent a decade working at a prestigious law firm, and it was there that he got his first taste of board dysfunction. In the course of his extensive executive career, Michael learned to identify and articulate some of the issues plaguing upper management, and he could see a better way for boards to operate. He felt that if he could sit on a board, rather than just report to it, he could make a substantial difference.

It was coming up on quitting time on a Friday afternoon in mid-September. There was a light rap on my door. Vita Pepe entered the room and told me that I was to clean out my desk and leave the building. It was an unceremonial end to a 15-year executive career.

It wasn't personal, but in the moment it certainly felt like it. A private equity firm, PEP, had taken control of the business earlier that day, and they had a fresh executive team waiting in the wings. I could take some solace in the fact that I was not the only one standing on the curb holding a box of my belongings, but despite this balm my cheeks and ears still burned.

When I look back on this moment now, I wish I could place a hand on my own shoulder and tell my younger self that they were actually doing me a good turn. My career as an executive was behind me, but a new and much-more-rewarding career was ahead of me.

Endnotes

1   Delizonna, L (2017) 'High-performing teams need psychological safety', *Harvard Business Review* (https://hbr.org/2017/08/high-performing-teams-need-psychological-safety-heres-how-to-create-it).

2   Fei, FX; Morris, A (2020) 'Begin with trust', *Harvard Business Review* (https://hbr.org/2020/05/begin-with-trust).

3   Gevurtz, Franklin A (2004) 'The Historical and Political Origins of the Corporate Board of Directors', *Hofstra Law Review*, Vol 33, Issue 1

4   Charan, R; Carey, D; Useem, M (2014) *Boards That Lead: When to Take Charge, When to Partner, and When to Stay Out of the Way*, Harvard Business Review Press.

5   Ibid.

6   ASX Corporate Governance Council (2019) *Corporate Governance Principles and Recommendations*, 4th edition (https://www2.asx.com.au/about/regulation/asx-corporate-governance-council).

7   Chiro, G (2018) 'The 6 ways to grow a company', *Harvard Business Review* (https://hbr.org/2018/06/the-6-ways-to-grow-a-company).

8   Gino, F (2018) 'The business case for curiosity', *Harvard Business Review* (https://hbr.org/2018/09/the-business-case-for-curiosity).

9   Latimer, D; Hodkinson C (2021) 'Corporate governance: A tale of three industries' (https://www2.deloitte.com/au/en/blog/risk-advisory-blog/2021/corporate-governance-tale-three-industries.html).

10 Cooperrider, D; Selian, A, Eds (2021) *The Business of Building a Better World: The Leadership Revolution That Is Changing Everything*, Random House.

11 Porter, ME (2021) 'The changing role of business in society' working paper (https://www.hbs.edu/ris/Publication%20Files/20210716%20Business%20in%20Society%20Paper%20For%20Website_84139c25-9147-4137-9ae9-28e27e1710a1.pdf).

12 Business Council of Australia (2021) Mission (https://www.bca.com.au).

13 Korn/Ferry International (2012) 'Cultivating greatness in the boardroom: What makes an exceptional non-executive director in Australasia?' (http://risk4good.com/wp-content/uploads/2011/08/KornFerry_Greatness-Cultivated-in-the-Boardroom-publication_2012.pdf).

14 Kiel, N (2021) 'How to…manage an underperforming director', *Company Director Magazine* (https://aicd.companydirectors.com.au/membership/company-director-magazine/2021-back-editions/august/how-to).

15 Ibid.

16 Latimer, D; Hodkinson C (2021) 'Corporate governance: A tale of three industries' (https://www2.deloitte.com/au/en/blog/risk-advisory-blog/2021/corporate-governance-tale-three-industries.html).

17 Motto, M (2021) 'Governance dysfunction and imploding boards: A rocky start to 2021' (https://www.governanceinstitute.com.au/news-media/news/2021/feb/governance-dysfunction-and-imploding-boards-a-rocky-start-to-2021/).

18 Hyland, A (2021) 'Board games: Is a cosy directors club a risk to corporate Australia?', *Sydney Morning Herald* (https://www.smh.com.au/business/companies/board-games-is-a-cosy-directors-club-a-risk-to-corporate-australia-20210906-p58p4z.html).

[19] Cunningham, L (2017) 'Warren Buffet's 10 commandments on board-room power and success', CNBC (https://www.cnbc.com/2017/07/17/warren-buffetts-10-commandments-on-boardroom-power-and-success.html?utm_content=buffer6484e&utm_medium=social&utm_source=twitter.com&utm_campaign=buffer).

[20] Churchill, N and Lewis, V (1983) 'Five stages of small business growth', *Harvard Business Review* (https://hbr.org/1983/05/the-five-stages-of-small-business-growth).

[21] Charan, R; Carey, D; Useem, M (2014) *Boards That Lead: When to Take Charge, When to Partner, and When to Stay Out of the Way*, Harvard Business Review Press.

Acknowledgements

The business mentors and leaders I admire are too many to list, and apologies to those not mentioned here.

Iconic Melbourne businessmen such as Ron Evans, Brian Blythe and Brendon O'Brien guided my executive career, whilst Ben Frenkel, George Kefford, Isaac Apel and Simon Feingold ushered me through the legal years.

I want to thank Michael Naphtali, Ross Johnston and Ian Roberts for sound counsel in my early years of transitioning from full-time executive into the Board portfolio life.

To my lifelong friends, Cromwell club members, and those family businesses I have worked with, a big thank you.

Last but not least, my two gorgeous daughters, Emily and Jasmine—you constantly remind me that all the problem-solving skills acquired in business are useless when navigating modern-day teenage years.

I give a special acknowledgment to Dr Jackie King, who drove the process that allowed me to complete this book, providing constructive feedback and input every step of the way. Jackie is an accomplished lawyer, academic and adviser on the interface between social issues and the commercial world. Her expertise is in social innovation, diversity, ethics, responsibility and sustainability. She is a trained LGBQTI+ ally.